CLOSE

LEADING WELL ACROSS
DISTANCE AND CULTURES

BY KEN COCHRUM

Published in eBook format by www.CreateSpace.com.
ISBN: 1492922005
ISBN 13: 9781492922001

WHAT OTHERS ARE SAYING ABOUT *CLOSE*

"As a cutting edge global leader, Ken's insights into the challenges and solutions posed by both distance and culture are excellent. Anyone striving to lead globally would be well served learning from this veteran practitioner."

MICHAEL SPRAGGINS, CEO of Spraggins Inc. and Chairman of LifeNet International

"Leading well, and developing other leaders, is hard enough when you only have to walk down the hallway to complete the task. But leading across many miles and over barriers of language and culture can feel utterly overwhelming. In *Close*, Ken Cochrum speaks with authority on the subject of leadership. He himself is an exceptionally strong leader, and he has invested his life in developing other leaders, both close at hand and across great distance. It has been observed that the Church will only rise to the level of its leadership. Ken helps us to raise the level of our own effectiveness in a new era of global leadership challenges. I am grateful for his insights shared in this book, and especially for his investment in my own life."

Dr. BRIAN G. FISHER, Senior Pastor, Grace Bible Church

"Through his years of leading across distance and culture, Ken Cochrum has gained unique perspective on what leading well looks like. In *Close: Leading Well across Distance and Cultures* Ken blends practical insights with rich theory and research, and provides essential advice for today's leaders. Globalization and the associated technological advances have brought the cultures and peoples of the world together. Ken provides guidance for navigating this new world of leadership effectively. It's my pleasure to commend Ken and this resource as you seek to engage the leadership opportunities before you."

JUSTIN A. IRVING, Ph.D., Director, Doctor of Ministry & Professor of Ministry Leadership, Bethel University

"Ken is a man of personal and professional excellence. In *Close* he has written a thoughtful and well-researched book that is grounded in his own extensive experience of learning and leading large. Ken is master of converting complex topics into practical actions that empower leaders. I highly recommend anything Ken writes."

HOLLY SHELDON, International Missionary for 26 years, Executive Director of 100%Sent Initiative, Cru

"*Close* is a *must-have* for everybody leading in this 21st century social media society. It is an excellent, easy-to-read book about leadership in a natural way. It shows the "how to's" and it is an amazing asset to look at what happens in the world as an opportunity and not as a threat. Ken is a person who leads by example. I have had the privilege to see him act as a *vulnerable, authentic* and *flexible* leader. Just read and practice this book to learn how to lead by *influencing.*"

JAN-WILLEM BOSMAN, Executive Leader of Jesus.net, Agape Netherlands

"In this quick-to-read and clear-to-grasp book, Ken, my friend and teammate, presents a distilled essence of leading over distance and across cultures. True to his ability to communicate complex issues in simple terminologies, in this book, Ken has skillfully integrated his global missionary and leadership experiences of over 20 years, the essential findings of his doctoral thesis, and some important biblical principles of leadership. As we lead in this fast-paced and more global-ized 21st century environment, *Close* helps us overcome the challenges of distance, culture, and resources so that we are more effective in our leadership."

Dr. BEKELE SHANKO, Vice President, Campus Crusade for Christ, Global Church Movements

CONTENTS

TABLES AND FIGURES

To Ann

INTRODUCTION

Why I Wrote This Book

The journey began when my wife Ann and I took our two young children, packed eleven suitcases, said goodbye to Texas, and moved to East Asia to launch a new venture. We had responded to a challenge to establish Christian movements among students on ten top-tier campuses in five gateway cities within five years. This was pioneering, pure and simple.

When I asked basic questions, such as, "How many people will we be given to start this venture?" or, "How much money is available?" the answers from our leaders were the same: whatever God enables you to raise. Slowly at first, then steadily, God stirred hearts. People joined with us and funds materialized.

Within three years several hundred coworkers came through those five sprawling urban centers. Some stayed for a few weeks, others for several years. They hailed from diverse nations such as Malaysia, Singapore, South Korea, and the USA. With each fresh face came fresh challenges. Most people didn't know the language. Many had very limited ministry skills. They understood less about our host culture and audience than we did.

Travel between cities was inconvenient and expensive. Tight security required constant vigilance in phone conversations, texts, and e-mails. Everyone had to be very careful with their communication, which was often in their second or even third language. This climate often left many of our staff feeling isolated, lonely, or disconnected. In a few cases team unity broke down, causing wonderful people to leave the field.

I vividly recall the day that Brian, a member of our small regional leadership team, had an "aha!" moment. "These courageous coworkers can't just be assigned and released into field ministry," he said. "If our mission is going to succeed, they need ongoing training, development, feedback and encouragement. They need… leadership."

It seems obvious now. But the leadership they needed was more than the face-to-face, see-you-at-our-next-staff-meeting style of shepherding in which I had been trained. The leadership they needed required more than classic vision casting, inspiration, strategy formulation, problem solving, and delegation. The leadership they needed couldn't be delivered in an annual field visit. They needed more.

They needed to be led – and loved – over distance. This book is the result of that two-decade journey.

At the time I did not know this challenge would become inextricably woven into my life's calling: to serve and strengthen Jesus Christ's leaders in our common mission.

To back up just a bit, cross-cultural leadership was a role into which I had been thrust at the tender age of twenty-three, with just one year as a staff member of Cru (the name of Campus Crusade for Christ in the United States) under my belt. I was entrusted with my first real team leader role—a six-month Short Term International mission project (STINT) in East Asia. It was scary and thrilling. By God's grace the team survived and we saw some lasting fruit.

I've been leading teams ever since. Along the way God has provided some amazing teammates. Since 1995 my full-time responsibilities have included leading people from diverse cultural backgrounds over vast distances. Through the years our teams have comprised women and men from the global east, west, north, and south. Nearly half of my ministry career was spent under a Singaporean leader who reported to a Korean who reported to an Indian.

For seven years I lived in Singapore, leading a twenty-five-member leadership team responsible for over a thousand missionaries in thirty-five cities throughout East Asia. Members on that team came from seven different countries and ranged from twenty-one-year-old accountants to grandparents in their mid-fifties.

This cross-cultural journey has included seasons of personal success and failure, emotional depression and feelings of inadequacy, mistakes and misunderstandings, high points and hard lessons. Sometimes these lessons were learned at a high cost to the relationships involved.

Since 2006 I have served as a vice president with Cru on our organization's Global Executive Team. I am responsible for providing spiritual and strategic leadership toward a global scope. One lesson I've learned is no matter what a person's level in an organization, or how broad one's scope, great leaders always long for more time with the people they have been called to lead.

Unfortunately, our fast-paced, highly mobile culture can work against our desires for intentional personal interaction. As leaders we can feel overwhelmed by expectations—real or perceived—to be available 24/7/365, to respond to every text and e-mail, to take time to connect relationally with key people in our social networks, and to do this across national borders and time zones. These forces conspire to spread our valuable attention miles wide and millimeters deep, ultimately satisfying no one. There simply isn't enough time to do it all.

Who is This Book For?

This book specifically seeks to help Christian leaders who are called to serve and lead across geographic and cultural barriers every day. You'll find help here if you:

- lead or participate in a distributed team, or multiple teams

- regularly collaborate through virtual work groups or task forces

- shepherd a multicultural or multigenerational team

- pastor a large or multi-site church

- regularly wrestle with expansive scope, steep learning curves, and rapidly changing environments

- provide mid- to high-level leadership in a complex multinational organization or company

- oversee a missions program or an international school

- serve as a board member or elder in any institution with the characteristics listed above

Do We Really Need Another Book on Leadership?

Current leadership literature is legion. As I surveyed publications helpful to Christian leaders, the vast majority addressed one of three audiences: (1) followers of Jesus currently leading or aspiring to lead within their local church; (2) business leaders whose virtual/distributed team models are driven primarily by a profit motive; (3) Christians seeking to apply biblical leadership principles within their home and work settings.

However, I couldn't locate a single book that would help leaders who are new to *both* distance and cross-cultural leadership climb the steep learning curve they face.

I've met a number of other leaders along the way who have encountered similar challenges and asked similar questions. The lack of easily accessible resources on this complex topic prompted me to invest three years in thesis research on servant leadership across distance and cultures. My desire is that these pages will provide help and hope for my brothers and sisters who wholeheartedly embrace God's call to global leadership.

What's Inside?

Your time is valuable. While the chapters are organized to flow logically, a brief summary of the entire book is provided below for those who like to skip directly to whatever they find most interesting.

Part 1 sets the context for global leadership. Chapter 1 explores the nature of the five-day leadership challenge. Most global leaders get no more than a total of 40 hours *per year* of face-to-face and phone/online contact with those they lead. How does one empower another to lead effectively the other 360 days per year? Chapter 2 looks at the current reality of the changing nature of global leadership in the 21st century. It gives us hard data that defines the work environment and its impact on workers. Chapter 3 calls us back to the scope of global leadership to which we are called by God in the midst of the existing culture. Chapter 4 surveys how the apostle Paul practiced servant leadership across distance and cultures during the rapid expansion of the first century church and gave us a model to follow today.

Part 2 explores three significant factors that work against effective global leadership today: power, distance, and culture. It proposes a fresh, research-grounded paradigm for 21st century global leaders.

Chapter 5 summarizes discussions and interviews with 80 top leaders on what they really want and need from those who lead them. Chapter 6 proposes servant leadership as the primary means to overcome power issues based on leader egos (yours and theirs). Chapter 7 deals with overcoming physical and psychological distance, particularly through the wise use of technology and travel. Chapter 8 points out the challenges we face interacting across culture and gives us some framework from which to navigate these challenges sensitively. Each of these three chapters includes what we've learned from research among top leaders and organizations, some real-life examples, essential leader competencies, and a few highly recommended resources. Chapter 9 challenges you to reflect on how you will apply what you've learned.

I invite you to consider these conclusions with an open mind and heart. It's tempting, if you're a field leader, to dismiss the idea of "research" as too academic, birthed in the ivory tower. Don't succumb to that temptation! Listen and learn from other peers who faced similar challenges.

If you have been called to lead across distance and cultures, embrace the challenge. Invest energy to learn the new skillsets required to be effective. In doing so you will not only experience deeper personal satisfaction, you will become a channel of blessing to the nations.

I designed this book to be read on a two- or three-hour flight by busy executives and ministry leaders. To enhance readability, I've chosen to exclude academic-style citations in favor of a robust bibliography at the end. If you are still hungry for more and would like the entire body of research along with detailed references, you can download my doctoral thesis, *Servant Leadership Across Distance and Cultures: A New Paradigm for 21ˢᵗ Century Global Leaders,* under the "Downloads" tab on my blog, www.OnLeadingWell.com.

PART 1:
HOW CLOSE ARE WE?

1

CLOSE IN FIVE
DAYS A YEAR

"Spiritual leadership is moving people onto God's agenda."
—Henry Blackaby, *Spiritual Leadership*

"The building of global teams is, indeed, the most important
business challenge of the twenty-first century. Global success
is now impossible without such teams."
—Michael Marquardt and Lisa Horvath, *Global Teams*

I had invested one week of my time, spent well over a thousand dollars in air tickets and conference fees, and flown eight thousand miles to have this critical eyeball-to-eyeball, heart-to-heart meeting.

This was one of my first trips in my new job as a strategy vice-president. I was charged with influencing James, an area strategy leader, toward greater ministry fruitfulness. James's direct boss, Aaron, and I did not see eye to eye. Our schedule only allowed ninety minutes for lunch, during which we had several important issues to discuss and come to agreement on so that James could freely do his job.

As Aaron and I sat down for this crucial conversation his wife Renee joined us. I was glad: she was delightful, engaging, and as good a storyteller as her husband. Twenty minutes later I glanced at my watch—time was flying by. We only had an hour left, but I figured that should still allow plenty of time to cover the agenda points both of us had laid out beforehand.

We sat at one of the few remaining open tables, which was a little too close to the buffet line. Naturally, people felt obliged to say hello. Some asked for a photo with them. Others sought a drive-by problem solving session, prefaced with an "I don't mean to interrupt you, but…" Finally the dining area thinned out and Renee excused herself to join a friend for coffee. We now had ten good minutes to address two major issues that would affect James's future and our mission effectiveness in this part of the world.

Was it worth it? You might be asking that, and as I settled into my airplane seat for the long journey home, I was provoked to ask it too. Did this trip really achieve what our mission demanded? What difference would this trip make, really, in the day-to-day work of Aaron, James, and their teams? Will I become another "out of sight, out of mind" leader in their busy worlds? Was this major investment of time and money for what seemed like a minimal return any way to lead a global organization? I found myself praying, "Lord, might there be a better way? Surely someone else has figured this out!"

* * *

Leadership is influence.

Spiritual leadership is spiritual influence. I like the way Henry Blackaby defines spiritual leadership as "moving people onto God's agenda." Blackaby's definition seems simple, but it has profound implications for you in your leadership role.

Good leaders are hard-wired to lead. A senior leader who is overseeing people and strategy in multiple locations has presumably been placed there because he or she can deliver results without requiring constant supervision.

Let's say you are responsible for leading a distributed team. Francis, a member of your team, lives four time zones away in Mali. Though French is her first language, she works well in English. Francis is sharp, dedicated, and a key contributor. Most days she wakes up, seeks the Lord, and then does what she feels like doing. She is setting an agenda. If you're leading her, your job is to help her *desire* to do what is both right and necessary...365 days per year. Your job is to help move and keep Francis on God's agenda.

But you're not in contact with her very often. You both may be working off a shared set of organizational priorities, but her daily whirlwind of mini-crises can easily derail momentum between your regular check-ins. Like we said, Francis is going to lead. How do you bridge the gap to ensure she is leading in the right direction?

I am frequently invited to teach leadership seminars for executives, ministry directors, and senior managers. They are responsible for leading people they don't get to see everyday. In the first session I invite these leaders to perform an exercise to calculate how much actual face-to-face, phone, and mediated online communication (e.g. Skype) time they have with one of the key people they lead from a distance.

Take a moment and do the same thing for one of your significant leadership relationships. Think about one person you currently lead over distance. Make a rough guess at the total in-person time you share with this individual in the course of one year. Now, get out your calendar and a piece of scrap paper. Review the past 12 months and add up the actual hours you spent "with" that person in face-to-face meetings, on a field visit, in virtual online meetings, and in personal phone/online calls.

What was your total? How did that compare with your estimate?

Every time I lead this exercise I am surprised by the results. On average, pastors of multi-site churches, ministry leaders, and high-level executives estimate they spend between twenty and forty hours **per year** in intentional personal interaction with people they lead over distance. That's it. Occasionally someone will break into the fifty-hour per year range, but that is rare.

Added together, those typical hours amount to at most five days per year. That's not a lot of time. Yet the success of these leaders' churches or organizations may rely on this small period of time.

This common experience has birthed what I call The Five-Day Rule of Heart: If a global leader has no more than five days per year of intentional personal interaction with his or her co-laborers in a multi-national context, how can that leader appropriately serve, strengthen, inspire, align, equip, and coach those field leaders to live and lead well throughout the other 360 days?

2

CLOSE IN THE 21ST CENTURY

The world has changed dramatically in the past decade. The human race is rapidly becoming a more tightly knit global community. A dip in one country's economy can prompt falls across world markets before the next day's trading cycle. A technological explosion of mobile devices, social networking, and cloud computing has made the world seem smaller.

These shifts have changed the way people live, work, think, learn, and relate to family and friends. Our expectations have changed. Increasingly, we believe that information and people should be available on demand. A global economy with shrinking boundaries allows buyers and sellers to conduct business non-stop, 24/7/365. For an increasing number of consumers it is easier and cheaper to order books, bicycle parts, or Mother's Day gifts from a mobile phone than it is to wait until the next free weekend to shop in brick-and-mortar stores. If anyone doubts the far-reaching significance of these kinds of changes, they might ask any political leader of the dozen or so Mideast countries who have recently experienced the "Arab Spring" how his or her views on the power of social networking have changed.

Companies, institutions, nonprofits, churches, and mission agencies are all struggling to keep up with this pace of change. Many are rightly questioning whether the practices that made yesterday's leaders successful will still be helpful tomorrow. In *Leading Across Boundaries: Creating Collaborative Agencies in a Networked World,* Russell Linden comments, "The most significant challenges facing our society cannot be addressed by any one organization. They all require collaboration among many organizations."

If you have ever tried to collaborate with another team, company or organization you know how difficult this can be. It takes work, trust, communication, and focus to deliver a level of partnership Linden writes about. The people who can deliver these partnerships are even rarer.

Success for the New Global Manager: What You Need to Know to Work across Distances, Countries, and Cultures notes that a number of top global management teams share the opinion, "The greatest obstacle to global effectiveness is a shortage of people who are prepared to manage and thrive in this new business paradigm."

In the twenty-first-century workplace, technological advances force most organizations to embrace some form of distributed teaming. In fact, the presence of purely localized teams is decreasing. A study commissioned by Cisco reports the proportion of U.S. workers taking advantage of flexible work schedules has more than doubled since 1985. According to *Officing Today,* the market research firm IDT estimated the world's mobile worker population surpassed one billion in 2010, and that by 2013 fully one-third of all workers would be mobile (defined as someone who works at least ten hours per week away from his or her primary office—doing field supervision, sales, business travel, itinerant ministry, or service at a client's location) and using online computer connections when doing so.

Today's leader must embrace his or her role as change agent. This type of leadership, as explained by Michael Hammer in *Faster, Cheaper, Better*, "is about vision and commitment, but it is also about taking difficult and even painful steps to ensure your company gets to where it needs to be."

James Ware, Executive Director of The Future of Work, put it this way:

> "When team members are not co-located they typically have relatively independent personal lives and social support systems. Realistically, they just don't have as much in common. They go to different churches, synagogues, and mosques; they participate in different local town events; their children attend different schools and participate in different sports programs. And they just don't bump into each other at the grocery store or on the commuter trains and buses. And even if we continue to prefer face-to-face meetings, the hard reality is that they are becoming a smaller and smaller percentage of our work experience. We've all got to learn how to work effectively with people who are located in other places most—or even all—of the time."

The workplace has changed forever.

The nature of work—how relevant tasks get assigned and accomplished—has also changed. Clemons and Kroth, in *Managing the Mobile Workforce: Leading, Building, and Sustaining Virtual Teams*, identify some of the new paradigms employees, staff, volunteers, and organizational leaders must embrace in order to work effectively in the new global environment (see Table 1).

Table 1. The Changing Rules of Work

Old Rules	New Rules
Work is a physical place	Work is something you do or accomplish
Work takes place between 8 a.m. and 5 p.m.	Work takes place between the time when it is assigned and when it is due
Employees, staff, or volunteers need to be controlled	Employees, staff, or volunteers are responsible for results
Work must be completed where the worker (or formal leader) is located	Work (surgery, personal evangelism, follow-up, mentoring, leadership decision-making) can occur far from the worker's location
Relationships are limited to whom one can meet personally	People can interact online with almost anyone and develop deep relationships with others they have never met face-to-face

Adapted from David Clemons and Michael S. Kroth, *Managing the Mobile Workforce: Leading, Building, and Sustaining Virtual Teams* (McGraw-Hill, 2011), 41.

Many already practice some of the new rules as individuals. For instance, the use of e-mail and Skype to support ministry interaction is nothing new. Also, a growing number of team members serving at a national, regional, or global level find themselves constantly depending upon telecommunications to include remote team members in meetings, planning, and ongoing relational connection.

Yet all too often institutions continue to organize, structure, and train employees and volunteers in ways that reflect the old rules and assumptions of work needing supervision. For instance, a team leader may feel pressure to require all team members to live in one city even though the team's charter includes a scope of ten or twenty countries. Or, current human resource policies may reveal the assumption that supervisory roles must continually interact face-to-face in order to effectively manage employees. But every global leader's philosophy, practice, and policy must reflect the new reality: work has become people-centric, not place-centric.

Effective spiritual leadership across distance and cultures is a crucial topic for all Christian missions right now, as the lines between local and global cultures blur, as the majority world surpasses North America in sending missionaries, as hierarchical organizations flatten into peer networks, and as a new generation of volunteers and full-time laborers assume responsibility for the Great Commission.

We have been wrestling with these issues for some time in Cru. In the sixty-plus years since Dr. Bill Bright founded the organization on the UCLA campus in southern California, it has grown to comprise dozens of different types of ministries led by staff or volunteers in almost every nation of the world. God has honored our commitment to raise indigenous national leaders and rapidly entrust them with overall responsibility for their nation's mission by weaving together a beautiful multinational tapestry. The forces of distance, culture, and power pull at the threads of that tapestry every day.

In the weeks after my visit with Aaron, my questions would not go away. I would come to find my experience was not uncommon. The challenges resonated with those I had the privilege of meeting through years of distance leadership. Yet when I looked for help from them, I found most did not have firm answers but were asking the same questions.

This launched me on a personal research project where I conducted in-depth interviews with more than twenty global leaders, and engaged another fifty top leaders in small-group discussions. I asked them how they dealt with leading, or being led, over distance. I also benefitted from feedback and comments collected from a global survey of 8,200 of our organization's staff members serving in over 150 nations.

I looked at best practices among global companies and non-profits that work across time zones and multiple cultures, and I studied biblical practices and principles that have worked over the past two thousand years.

Here's what I learned: global leadership is difficult!

Surprised? Of course not. No one is born knowing how to do all this. But we need to consider the impact of our shortcomings. I made a lot of mistakes that cost me relational trust. It cost my team and organization time, money, and emotional energy that could have yielded greater fruit with fewer bruised relationships along the way.

My research and study revealed more, though. I discovered what top leaders really want from those to whom they report and are responsible. And I identified three specific shifts in mindset and competencies you need to lead well across distance and cultures. They provide a new paradigm for leading effectively in the twenty-first century.

However, before we look to the results, it is important to revisit our call to participate in this global culture.

3

THE INEVITABILITY OF BEING CLOSE

Go and make disciples of all nations.
- Jesus

When multiplying disciples are present everywhere – geo-graphically, culturally, and linguistically – that doesn't just make fulfilling the Great Commission possible, it makes it inevitable!
- Steve Douglass, President of Cru

After this I looked, and behold, a great multitude that no one could number, from every nation, from all tribes and peoples and languages, standing before the throne and before the Lamb
- Revelation 7:9 (ESV)

The challenges and complexities of leadership in the 21st century are daunting, yet our mission to press on amidst these realities has been clear from the beginning. When the resurrected Jesus Christ authoritatively commissioned his small band of followers to go and make disciples of all nations he fully expected them and their spiritual offspring to complete the task.

Jesus's expectation was not based on the disciples' propensity to obey, nor their track record of successful ministry. Rather, his expectation was grounded in something much more profound: the boundless love of God and his desire to be named and glorified among all nations.

My friend Paul Eshleman understands this well. In the late 1970's, Paul accepted a challenge from Bill Bright to put the story of Jesus into a movie format so that more people would be able to see and understand God's love for them. Paul spearheaded production of the JESUS film, which, as of this writing, has been translated into 1,188 languages and viewed by 6 billion people from every nation in the world. Paul understands global scope.

I've enjoyed spending time with Paul in formal and informal settings over the past few years. No matter where our conversations begin, they always seem to come around to God's love for people and the fulfillment of the Great Commission.

> *Jesus' expectation was not based on the disciples' propensity to obey, nor their track record of successful ministry.*

One evening Ann and I were enjoying a relaxed dinner with Paul after a day filled with meetings. As we watched the sun set from a beachfront restaurant on Florida's Gulf coast, talk turned from family updates to God's plan for the nations. Paul began,

"Two thousand years ago, Jesus told us to take the Gospel to the whole world. He was very definite about it. In fact, He gave us the same command five different times in the first five books of the New Testament.

1.   Matthew 28:18-19 defines the **depth** of the Great Commission. "Then Jesus came to them and said, 'All authority in heaven and on earth has been given to me. Therefore, go and make disciples of all nations, baptizing them in the name of the Father and of the Son and of the Holy Spirit, teaching them to obey everything I have commanded you.'"

2.   Mark 16:15 emphasizes the **breadth** and **quantity** of the sowing. "He said to them, 'Go into all the world and preach the good news to all creation.'"

3.   Luke 24:46-47 shows the **surety** of the Great Commission. "He told them, 'This is what is written: The Christ will suffer and rise from the dead on the third day, and repentance and forgiveness of sins will be preached in His name to all nations, beginning at Jerusalem.'"

4.   John 20:21 shows Jesus as the **model** of the Great Commission. "Again Jesus said, 'Peace be with you! As the Father has sent me, I am sending you.'"

5. Acts 1:8 speaks of the **extent** of the Great Commission. "But you will receive power when the Holy Spirit comes on you; and you will be My witnesses in Jerusalem, and in all Judea and Samaria, and to the ends of the earth."

"Ken and Ann, the Great Commission tells us what we are to do and where. Jesus also gave us the Great Commandment, which tells us who we are to love and how.

"When Jesus was asked what the greatest commandment was, He replied, 'Love the Lord your God with all your heart, and with all your soul, and with all your mind, and with all your strength, and love your neighbor as yourself.' The second one was like it, 'to love your neighbor as yourself.' He also gave us clear commands as to the people we were to love: Love God (John 14:15). Love your neighbor (John 13:34). Love strangers (Matthew 25:35, 36). Love your enemies (Luke 6:27)."

Ann and I took a long walk on the beach that night before heading back to our hotel room. We reflected on the mentoring we'd just received. We prayed. As a new vice president stepping into a challenging global leadership role, Paul's words gave me clarity and hope. Yes, the world is a big, complex and confusing place. But the heart of God's call to us as global leaders is straightforward:

- Love God.
- Love people.
- Make disciples among every nation, language, tribe, and people group.
- All means all. Every means every.
- All followers of Jesus are expected to play a part.
- One day this task will be completed.
- It's inevitable.

Ann and I agreed, "OK. We're all in."

Our response that night wasn't something new to us. We had fully surrendered our lives to Jesus' direction many times before. However, we did sense freshness and renewal of our calling. We were grateful to be loved by a God with such a huge heart and an amazing plan for the nations. Why wouldn't we want to obey him to go anywhere, at anytime, to do anything, at any cost?

When I am frustrated at an apparent lack of progress in our mission, I am reminded that God will fulfill his plan in his way and in his time. He invites us to play our part in his mission. He invites us to lead well by loving well. Any attempt to shape God's leaders in the twenty-first century must be grounded with conviction of God's boundless love and in his ability to see his plan fulfilled.

It's inevitable.

4

PAUL: A PIONEER IN LEADING CLOSE

"For I want you to know how great a struggle I have for you
and for those at Laodicea and for all
who have not seen me face to face."
Colossians 2:1

We may consider the apostle Paul one of the world's first truly global leaders. In his lifetime, Paul crossed distance and culture, leading from the posture of a committed servant, in order to fulfill the Great Commission. His methods seemed radical to his contemporaries, but they were firmly grounded in God's biblical plan for His people.

Paul's Calling

In his letter to the Gentile church in Galatia, Paul reaches back across the centuries to Abraham, "And the Scripture, foreseeing that God would justify the Gentiles by faith, preached the gospel beforehand to Abraham, saying, 'In you shall all the nations be blessed'" (Galatians 3:8). Later Paul writes, "There is neither Jew nor Greek, there is neither slave nor free, there is no male and female, for you are all one in Christ Jesus. And if you are Christ's, then you are Abraham's offspring, heirs according to promise" (Galatians 3:28-29).

Paul argues that God's promises confirm two truths. First, God remains in sovereign control of his plan to bless all nations. Second, the good news of Jesus Christ was not just for Jews back then or for Christians today. It transcends all ethnic, economic, cultural, and gender boundaries.

Paul unpacks the mystery most clearly in his letter to the church he helped plant among Gentiles in Ephesus:

> When you read this, you can perceive my insight into the mystery of Christ, which was not made known to the sons of men in other generations as it has now been revealed to his holy apostles and prophets by the Spirit. *This mystery is that the Gentiles are fellow heirs, members of the same body, and partakers of the promise in Christ Jesus through the gospel.* Of this gospel I was made a minister according to the gift of God's grace, which was given me by the working of his power (Ephesians 3:4-7, emphasis added).

What had not been known in prior generations was now revealed: that the Gentiles and Jews are together in Christ Jesus. Paul uses three compound nouns—fellow heirs, members, and partakers—to specify this togetherness, all of which begin with the Greek prefix *syn*, meaning with or together. This tri-fold "withness" in Christ was available only through the gospel.

Paul's position shocked both Jews and Gentiles. These two groups had hated each other for generations. Hearts hardened by pride and ethnocentrism blinded the Jews to the larger plan of God for all nations. Like antibodies fighting an intruder in the body, the prevailing Jewish culture rejected an interpretation of prophecy that did not support their narrow point of view. The Gentiles were shocked because after centuries of being looked down by the Jews, they now heard the good news that they had been grafted in to God's family. They were equals. Paul was telling both groups that everything had changed— Old Testament prophecies of the salvation of the Gentiles were fulfilled by Jesus' death and resurrection.

The friction caused by his message brought trouble for Paul and his band of church-planting missionaries. Paul wrote to the church in Ephesus as a prisoner for Christ Jesus on behalf of the Gentiles. Of this gospel, he said, "I was made a minister [Greek *diakonos*, or servant] according to the gift of God's grace ... to preach to the Gentiles the unsearchable riches of Christ, and to bring to light for everyone what is the plan of the mystery hidden for ages in God" (Ephesians 3:7-9).

Paul's trials remind us that there is a cost to taking the gospel across distance and cultures, but in light of God's calling and plan for the nations, it was a cost he and his co-laborers were gladly willing to pay.

Paul viewed his ministry as a continuation of what Jesus began in bringing salvation to all nations. He stated this point clearly after he and Barnabas were sent out from Antioch to preach the gospel in Pisidian Antioch (Acts 13:13-52). Adhering to their typical strategy of going "to the Jew first" in synagogues (Rom. 1:16), their first round of preaching was well received by Jews and converts to Judaism. They were invited back for another hearing. When they returned the following Sabbath, the Jews grew jealous; they reviled Paul and his message. After being rejected,

> Paul and Barnabas spoke out boldly, saying, "It was necessary that the word of God be spoken first to you. Since you thrust it aside and judge yourselves unworthy of eternal life, behold, we are turning to the Gentiles. For so the Lord has commanded us, saying, 'I have made you a light for the Gentiles, that you may bring salvation to the ends of the earth'" (Acts 13:46-47).

Paul here quotes directly from Isaiah 61:1-2, bridging the gap between what Jesus had already accomplished and the remaining task of making disciples of all nations.

The results of turning from the Jews to the Gentiles were astonishing. "And when the Gentiles heard this, they began rejoicing and glorifying the word of the Lord, and as many as were appointed to eternal life believed. And the word of the Lord was spreading throughout the whole region" (Acts 13:48-49).

While testifying on trial in Acts 26, Paul relayed the story of his personal commissioning from Jesus: "But rise and stand upon your feet, for I have appeared to you for this purpose, to appoint you as a servant and witness to the things in which you have seen me and to those in which I will appear to you" (v.16).

It is important not to miss the connections in Paul's writing between:

- a sovereign God's loving plan for all nations

- the good news that salvation and freedom are only available through Jesus Christ

- Paul's role as a servant in bringing this good news to everyone, to the Jew first and also to the Greek

- suffering as a normal experience for those participating in God's mission

These themes permeate Paul's epistles. In order to accomplish his mission among the nations, God calls humble servants to preach good news of freedom from personal sin, institutional oppression, and religious burdens while personally suffering rejection and violence from many of their hearers.

Paul's Ministry

Paul's ministry was primarily cross-cultural and conducted over great distance. Roland Allen, an Anglican missionary to North Africa and China in the early 1900s, explains in *Missionary Methods: St. Paul's or Ours?* "In little more than ten years St. Paul established the Church in four provinces of the [Roman] Empire, Galatia, Macedonia, Achaia and Asia. Before AD 47 there were no churches in these provinces; in AD 57 St Paul could speak as if his work there was done."

Paul and his missionary teams traveled about twelve hundred miles as the crow flies from Jerusalem to Berea in Macedonia, one of their most remote areas of church planting. They covered great distances in relatively short periods of time, rarely lingering more than a few Sabbaths in any particular location. The exception to this was prolonged stays of roughly two years each in Corinth and Ephesus.

Paul's calling and burden was to preach the gospel of Jesus Christ to win as many Jews or Gentiles as possible (1 Corinthians 9:19-22), and to press on to locations where Christ had not yet been named (Romans 15:20-21). His ultimate goal was to plant churches by laying a foundation as a skilled master builder, leaving behind a healthy, growing community of new believers and leaders in each location who were grounded in theology and the ethics of the law-free gospel (1 Corinthians 3:6, 10; 9:10). His missionary strategy did not seem to be fully defined in fine detail, but was driven by desire to move from province to province with constant sensitivity to the Spirit's leading.

Paul's leadership was spiritual and strategic. Examples of his flexibility in following the Spirit include being sent out from Antioch in Acts 13:2-3, wanting to preach in Asia and Bithynia but being turned back by "the Spirit of Jesus" in Acts 16:6-7, and then receiving and responding to the Macedonian vision of a man urging the team to "come over to ... help us" in Acts 16:9-10.

The vast distances and long periods of time required for Paul and his co-laborers to travel as the Spirit led them is impressive. In *The Moody Atlas of Bible Lands*, Barry Beitzel observes:

> The distances traveled by the apostle Paul are nothing short of staggering. In point of fact, the New Testament registers the equivalent of about 13,400 airline miles that the great apostle journeyed; and if one takes into account the circuitous roads he necessarily had to employ at times, the total distance traveled would exceed that figure by a sizable margin. Moreover it appears that the New Testament does not document all of Paul's excursions... Considering the means of transportation available in the Roman

world, the average distance traveled in a day, the primitive paths, and rugged sometimes mountainous terrain over which he had to venture, the sheer expenditure of the apostle's physical energy becomes unfathomable for us. Many of those miles carried Paul through unsafe and hostile environs largely controlled by bandits who eagerly awaited a prey (cf. 2 Corinthians 11:26). Accordingly, Paul's commitment to the Lord entailed a spiritual vitality that was inextricably joined to a superlative level of physical stamina and fearless courage.

Eckhard J. Schnabel would agree. In his excellent book *Paul the Missionary: Realities, Strategies and Methods*, Schnabel estimates that Paul journeyed a total of 15,500 miles (25,000 kilometers) over land and sea which would have required more than 660 days based on transportation methods of the day. In terms of distance, Paul surely understood global leadership.

Paul also understood the complexities of distance leadership. Paul would confront significant political, cultural, and linguistic barriers in most of the places he ministered. Rapid appointment of indigenous leaders in each location minimized cultural friction by ensuring that qualified, accepted insiders handled the primary functions of leadership (teaching, direction setting, shepherding, and conflict resolution). This strategy greatly increased Paul's capacity to influence hundreds and thousands, rather than merely tens and fifties—echoing Jethro's advice to Moses in Exodus 18:21-23. Jethro urged Moses to select leaders from every tribe based on character and competence, then let them decide all critical decisions. Acts 14:21-23 provides a snapshot of Paul's approach during his first missionary journey:

> When they had preached the gospel to that city and had made many disciples, they returned to Lystra and to Iconium and to Antioch, strengthening the souls of the disciples, encouraging them to continue in the faith, and saying that through many tribulations we must enter the kingdom of God. And when they had appointed elders for them in every church, with prayer and fasting they committed them to the Lord in whom they had believed.

Paul and Barnabas preached the gospel, made many disciples, and then focused on these new relationships by strengthening their souls, encouraging them, and telling them the honest truth about the suffering they would encounter. One can sense the balanced concern between cause and community, between mission and relationships. Paul and his teams were not interested in trying to maintain ongoing direct control over these nascent churches. They expected local disciples to learn to lead quickly.

Another example of Paul's capacity to build relationships and demonstrate love over distance may be found in Romans 16. Here Paul addresses twenty-seven people by name—many of them with great affection and knowledge of personal detail—*although he had not yet visited that city.* Clearly Paul understood the value of relationships. He mastered the skills of distance leadership in a common mission.

Rapid appointment of indigenous leaders in each location minimized cultural friction by ensuring that qualified, accepted insiders handled the primary functions of leadership.

One concise biblical example of servant leadership across distance and culture may be observed in Paul's approach to team ministry with Silas and Timothy in Thessalonica (Acts 17:1-9). The team appears to have spent only three weeks in Thessalonica, yet the seeds planted in this cross-cultural effort bore much lasting fruit. Their joint letter to the church there exemplifies team-based distance ministry focused on:

- hope in Jesus Christ (mentioned in every chapter)

- ministry in person, face-to-face (1 Thessalonians 1:5-6; 2:1-12)

- ministry through prayer (1:2; 3:6-13)

- ministry by proxy (sending Timothy when Paul could not go himself, 3:2, 6)

- ministry through the pen (5:27)

- shared leadership (Paul uses "we," "us," and "our" one hundred times, compared to only four uses of singular pronouns "I" or "me")

- mutual respect for others leaders (5:12-13)

- acknowledgement of their heart's "great desire to see you face to face" (2:17).

Anyone called to serve in global leadership will benefit from an in-depth study of this letter in its historical context.

The Bible tells us that there is nothing new under the sun (Ecclesiastes 1:9). While the specifics in our modern-day lives may be different than Paul's, the example he gave us demonstrates universal principles and truths that can help us today.

Paul's Principles

As a servant leader with a clear calling and vision for God's glory to be spread to all nations, Paul exhibited core aspects of servant leadership through his life, strategies, and methods. These qualities form the foundation for our growth as global leaders.

Calling

Paul viewed himself as called by God as a servant sent to proclaim the good news. Understanding and acceptance of one's calling provides a deep personal sense of security and emotional stability. This stable foundation allows one to freely serve others without risking personal worth. A clear sense of calling also provides motivation to endure through inevitable difficulty and suffering. Paul frequently referred to his calling and purpose in his letters (Romans 1:1-5, 15:20-21; 1 Corinthians 9:15-23).

Intimacy with God

Paul constantly affirmed and modeled the fundamentals of pursuing unbroken fellowship and abiding intimacy with God. These practices included devotion (2 Corinthians 11:3), intercessory prayer (Ephesians 1:15-23), and walking in the fullness of the Holy Spirit (Galatians 5:22-23). He knew that a servant's ministry shrivels up when an abiding first love for God is abandoned (Revelation 2:1-5).

Love

Paul constantly referred to the primacy of *agapao* love. Love was his dominant ethic—far above service, self-sacrifice, faith, or hope (1 Corinthians 13:1-8; Galatians 5:22-23). Paul's missionary teams were controlled by the love of Christ as they served as ambassadors in the ministry of reconciliation (2 Corinthians 5:14-21).

Humility

Humility is a dominant theme in the preaching and practice of Paul. The *Greek-English Lexicon of the New Testament and Other Early Christian Literature* defines humility as being "of low position, poor, lowly, undistinguished, of no account." Paul frequently spoke of the necessity of this trait (Acts 20:19; 2 Corinthians 10:1; 11:7; Ephesians 4:2; Philippians 2:3,8; Colossians 3:12). Humility is the opposite of pride, a servant leader's greatest enemy.

Zeal

Humble doesn't mean limp. It has been said that pride leads to fear, but humility leads to great boldness for Christ. This is often misunderstood among spiritual leaders. Paul manifested intense passion for God and his glory among the nations. Paul exhorted leaders to lead with zeal and not be slothful in zeal but fervent in spirit, serving the Lord (Romans 12:8, 11).

Empowerment

Paul invested in people as his primary strategy. He aggressively entrusted others with the mission. Paul also had clear selection criteria for his missionary teams and local church leaders (Acts 15:36-40; 2 Timothy 2:2; Titus 1:5-9, 2:2-10), and actively involved women in his ministry (Acts 16:13; Romans 16:3). He trained and released other leaders by sending them out (Acts 14:21-24; Titus 1:5). He prayerfully, intentionally, and strategically risked the future of the church by empowering others. Paul gave power away.

Vision

Paul constantly kept the big picture in front of his disciples and audiences. It seems he did this almost as a matter of fact, not because he was a great vision caster, but Paul assumed the whole world was always in view. He always had to get to the next frontier and he talked about this to his followers in normal conversation (e.g. Romans 15:24, 28 — he had to get to Spain). He took great pains in most of his letters and sermons to explain the big picture of God's plan before calling his audience to action with imperatives.

Service

Paul makes a point to explain Jesus's example of service in Philippians 2:6-8, "he did not count equality with God a thing to be grasped, but made himself nothing, taking the form of a servant, being born in the likeness of men. And being found in human form, he humbled himself by becoming obedient to the point of death, even death on a cross." Paul exemplified this in his own life. He set aside legitimate personal rights in order to minister more effectively to people from diverse cultural backgrounds, and sought to make himself a servant to all.

> For though I am free from all, I have made myself a servant to all, that I might win more of them. To the Jews I became as a Jew, in order to win Jews. To those under the law I became as one under the law (though not being myself under the law) that I might win those under the law. To those outside the law I became as one outside the law (not being outside the law of God but under the law of Christ) that I might win those outside the law. To the weak I became weak, that I might win the weak. I have become all things to all people, that by all means I might save some. I do it all for the sake of the gospel, that I may share with them in its blessings (1 Corinthians 9:15, 18-23).

Suffering

Paul understood the role that suffering would play in taking the good news to the nations. He directly connected his servanthood to his suffering through great labors, imprisonments, countless beatings, near death experiences, being stoned, being in danger from robbers and false brothers, toil and sleeplessness, hunger and thirst, and above all else, his daily concern for young churches (2 Corinthians 11:23 – 28). He willingly risked inconvenience, rejection of his message, pain, suffering, and his own life in order to advance God's mission.

Results

Lasting fruit glorifies God (John 15:8, 16). Paul left in his wake a growing community of loyal, trusting friends who were committed to following Jesus Christ at great personal cost. He completed his time on earth having accomplished the work God had given him to do (2 Timothy 4:6-8). He touched lives, made disciples, preached to prisoners and kings, and raised men and women who planted an unstoppable worldwide movement that continues bearing fruit today.

We are not the first to face the challenge of caring for, shepherding, and directing those who may be far away. Paul is just one example of a leader who modeled principles of leading across geographical and cultural distance in response to God's call. Ministry in the twenty-first century will require character-grounded, innovative servant leaders who can flex with God's Spirit, and who are comfortable leading over greater distances with less control over God's people. These principles form the backbone of our new paradigm for 21st century global leaders.

PART 2: GETTING CLOSE

5

WHAT CLOSE
LOOKS LIKE

Ask any veteran "what do leaders really do?" and you'll get a fairly predictable set of responses. You'll probably hear that good leaders cast vision and set direction, inspire and motivate, align and communicate, coach and delegate. They listen well and involve others before making final decisions. Dozens of "How To" leadership books are published each year that repackage those skills in an attempt to help leaders improve.

What if we asked a different question?

What if we asked veteran leaders, "How do you want to be led?"

During the past two years I had the opportunity to interact with 80 of my organization's top global leaders who represent every area of the world. Most of these men and women have served for over 15 years in some type of distance leadership involving oversight of strategies in multiple countries. The majority has lived outside their home nation for five years or longer. They help set long-term direction for our organization and are responsible for moving the mission forward in over 160 nations.

Here are five consistent replies that surfaced from the interviews.

Leaders want respect. Though respect is conferred differently in various cultures, people always appreciate graciousness, honor, and appropriate deference to their experience. Mature leaders don't demand respect, rather they exude a gravitas of character and humble confidence that reflects wisdom. *Each person is worth listening to.*

Leaders want understanding and empathy. These women and men have difficult jobs. They travel a lot. Their time is stretched thin. They are doing their best to find rhythm between work, home, church, and a meaningful social life. Often they have few true peers that live nearby. Their vision typically outstrips their resources by a factor of ten or a hundred. Remember these pressures in conversations when you're evaluating someone's effectiveness, or asking them to consider taking on a new project. *Get on the same emotional page.*

Leaders want to be led by someone honest, authentic, and competent. People don't expect their leaders to be perfect – but they do expect them to be honest. They want to see leaders respond authentically, sharing about their own failures and successes. They want to see their leaders growing in competencies that help them do their jobs well, and thus improve the overall organization. Few of those I spoke with, if any, mentioned that they wanted to have their direction set, their strategies formulated, or needed to be motivated by more words from leaders above them. *If that's not what people want from their leaders, why assume that you should be giving those you lead more of this type of leadership?*

Leaders want a clear challenge to contribute to the organization's purpose. That's why most of them signed on. They want more clarity on the *whats* of the mission, not the *hows*. They'll figure out how to get there. They want to be entrusted with more. *What they need from me is an* **appropriate challenge, consistent support,** *and* **honest feedback** *on how they're doing.*

Leaders want to share leadership. This fascinated me, as when our organization restructured recently, one of the five principles guiding our efforts was "shared leadership." Many leaders initially resisted this, claiming that the essence of leadership—at least in their culture—was having someone in charge to make the final decisions. Yet people don't want to be led that way. They want to voice their opinions. They want to help shape overall direction. They long for the dynamic interaction among leader-followers that characterizes high performance teams. They want to be engaged in issues and decisions that they will ultimately own. *They long to share leadership.*

Four Practices of Leading Close

In addition to these five common desires, four dominant practices emerged from my extended conversations that reflect how these men and women lead well across distance and cultures. Not surprisingly, two themes focus on their relationships and two focus on the mission. They were:

1. Effective leaders have a big heart to care for people. They love well.

Leadership is fundamentally a relationship that must exhibit genuine care and concern for those being led. One leader expressed the need to build relationships this way: "You have to establish a really solid sense of relationship that is based on the heart. That is the most important thing, yet one of the things we're less focused on cultivating. When I go to teams and talk to them about their hearts I watch their eyes open up, and it's like a physical reaction to being viewed as a soul, as a heart, rather than as a transactional leader whose job is to execute the organizational priorities."

Another said: "You have to genuinely care about the people that you're supposed to be exercising servant leadership over. Are they people that you're willing to commit to on a personal level? Second, you have to believe in them and give them opportunities to lead as opposed to trying to control them over distance. If you have to try to control them, you have the wrong person in the job. You have to give them freedom to lead, otherwise you're not really serving them; you're serving your own need to control."

An inevitable challenge to this is one's personal relationship capacity. Building relationships requires time. Although telecommunications technology and social networking tools enable people to connect with almost anyone at any time, this technology has not enabled the heart to have the same capacity to listen, empathize, and genuinely care for hundreds or thousands of individuals. This relates to the second theme:

2. Effective distance leaders practice consistent two-way communication that leads to mutual respect, trust, and understanding.

Establishing trust was consistently mentioned in my interviews as a key element of success. Trust develops as one experiences genuine concern and advocacy from one's leaders. Leaders said they built trust through service, listening, visiting and humbly seeking to understand in different ways.

"Make sure you're going to their turf, not always expecting them to come to you," said one.

"Consistent calls make deposits of trust with the people you're leading at a distance," said another. "I spend a lot more time listening to them as opposed to telling them what to do."

A third told me: "Understanding is key. For me that means I understand what's happening in their space. For them it means they have someone who knows them, outside of their team setting, that they can talk with that is fighting for them. An advocate. A safe place to process where the essentials are already aligned."

To overcome the distance barrier, distance leaders noted, they had to raise their level of intentionality in scheduling interactions. One commented: "I have learned I need a plan to initiate contact regularly and put it as a priority. If not, I just get busy and focus on urgent things."

In terms of working with technology, one leader asked: "What is needed? You need a tech platform that just works. We don't want to blow the time messing with technology. Once you have bandwidth, audio, or tech problems, the tech is no longer transparent – then you can't focus on the person and the issues. It's like we're looking through a window. We can't clink glasses, but we can really communicate. Once the window's dirty, we begin focusing on the medium, the specks on the window, instead of the person and the message."

Another leader underscored the importance of using technology well. "We need understanding and simplicity in our communications," he said. "A loving and caring environment must be there. Distance leadership can easily lack this element. We must take time to know the personal aspects of a leader. Offline communication (using email, Facebook, a handwritten letter) must be very good, and online (Skype, video conference, phone) must also be good. Face-to-face communication must not be forgotten!"

3. Effective distance leaders help others stay focused on the mission and critical tasks.

Several leaders mentioned the need to clarify their message and remain focused on the mission in their communications. By emphasizing mission they were not minimizing the need to build relationships. However, once relational trust is in place, mission clarity becomes top priority.

Said one: "I am very specific and focused about what we're talking about and what we're doing together. I would tend to say, let's talk about fewer things more deeply. Get them to do a few things really, really well, but keep them growing in their capacity to do and juggle other things so that they can delegate."

The most effective leaders and teams exercise discipline in limiting agendas to the most essential items. Fully exploring and completing one or two topics per call gives everyone a sense of positive momentum that builds expectations for the next call. Long, unfinished agendas are depressing and make meetings feel like a waste of precious time.

4. Effective distance leaders add value by providing relevant help and resources.

Servant leadership involves helping others grow and develop while achieving their goals. The millennial generation expects their leaders to be concerned about their goals. Often this point is neglected because leaders tend to assume that unless they hear otherwise, people have all they need within reach. Serving the field by providing timely help and resources is a challenging and essential aspect of effective distance leadership.

A follower should be able to identify specific ways that his or her leader added value or provided help. "There are a lot of assumptions when people are put into positions that simply aren't true," one leader told me. "We tend to assume spirituality and the gospel-oriented leadership, and we can't."

We need to dig.

This seems basic, but when pressed for time it is easy to forget to ask service-oriented questions. What can we ask about? Almost anything. Phillip, a leader in Southeast Asia, regularly asks, "Do you read or listen to other things? Are you available to grow? How are you and God? Are you experiencing joy in your heart? It's tough to get people to answer this honestly."

A New Paradigm

We want to feel connected to people we work with. We long to close the natural gaps created by position, distance, and culture. We need a new paradigm, one in which we are not focused on the distance that separates us, but on what brings us close.

This new paradigm gives us three main focal points: servant leadership, distance leadership, and cross-cultural leadership. These are the *whats* of leading close. Each focal point has a few essential characteristics or competencies. These are research-grounded *hows* that guide our actions to grow as global leaders. Table 2 lays out the paradigm.

It's important to note that this paradigm can sit on top of your organization's current leadership framework. You probably already have a way of thinking about leadership that deals with important matters such as the heart, prayer, selection, character development, competency training, experience, exposure, and regular feedback. This paradigm isn't meant to replace that, but to provide additional support for leaders with highly complex roles.

Table 2. A New Paradigm for Leading Close

Aspect	Essential Characteristics and Competencies
Servant leadership	1. Fully embraces God's call to global level leadership of the organization 2. Increases in virtues of *agapao* love, humility, altruism, vision, trust, empowerment, and service 3. Listens in order to understand and empathize 4. Embraces suffering (pruning, pain, rejection, increased criticism, and misunderstanding) 5. Shares leadership; follows and leads equally well
Distance leadership	1. Leads a stable personal life 2. Able to leverage face-to-face and mediated communication to rapidly build trusting relationships 3. Able to assert authority without being overbearing, inflexible, or controlling; mentors with empathy 4. Global thinker; able to solve increasingly complex problems and offer flexibility in local implementation 5. Able to build virtual teams that connect people, manage information, and execute action across borders

Cross-cultural leadership	1. Grows in self-awareness of personal cultural values and biases
	2. Demonstrates cultural interest, sensitivity, and adaptability
	3. Fosters mutuality and participation in all leadership venues
	4. Understands cultural indices' impact on strategy implementation and adjusts leadership appropriately

6

SERVE CLOSE

"A servant leader does what is necessary."
- framed on my desk

"My task was to visit a team in a country far from our area office and help them choose a leader. One of our standard exercises was to lead the team in an extended discussion of servant leadership, including both one-on-one and group interaction. We did this before opening the process of nominating candidates so that the team would have the right things in mind as they considered who should lead them. On this occasion we considered this discussion especially important, because the leading candidate was the acting team leader, a strong leader who didn't seem to include others in his decision-making and didn't seem to be a strong developer of younger leaders. Looking at him through my grid, I questioned whether he qualified as a servant leader."

Erick Schenkel, executive director of the JESUS Film project at Cru, shared this experience of his with me. Servant leadership is not a new concept. It has, however, drawn renewed interest in the past decade due in large part to the perceived underperformance of over-loaded institutional leaders who cannot possibly measure up to the traditional "leader as hero" model.

Servant leadership describes "those leaders who lead an organiza-tion by focusing on their followers," according to Kathleen Patterson, one of the pioneer thinkers in the recent field of servant leadership modeling and research. The term "servant leadership" was coined in 1970 by Robert Greenleaf, and expressed more fully in his seminal work, *Servant Leadership*. "The servant-leader is servant first," he wrote, going on to offer this test of servant leadership: "Do those served grow as persons? Do they, *while being served*, become healthier, wiser, freer, more autonomous, more likely themselves to become servants?"

Greenleaf observed that although ego drives achievement, ser-vant leaders must develop their followers by curbing their own egos, sharing power, and intentionally developing each of the relationships they have to help followers grow into equals. The leader then becomes the *primus inter pares*, or first among equals.

Steve Douglass, president of Cru, models this well. I've watched Steve as he has intentionally sought to grow in giving leadership away to his vice presidents on the executive team. Sharing leadership became a guid-ing principle when we restructured a few years ago. Steve models that in our executive team meetings by ensuring that the one who is ultimately responsible to implement something has the authority to raise the issue, guide the team's discussion, facilitate any decision-making process, and make the final decision. As team leader, Steve serves as first among equals in setting the pace and calling us to fulfill our organization's mission.

Recently, as part of their training in distance leadership, we had some other ministry leaders observe one of our executive team's weekly one-hour virtual meetings. They watched online as our team tackled a fairly significant issue. After Steve opened the meeting in prayer, Andrea, our VP for Leadership Development, led the team through a decision-making process that resulted in a clear pathway forward. During the feedback session, several observers noted their surprise that the president didn't really say much, but let the team work through various viewpoints, then supported Andrea's final decision. This is servant leadership at the highest level.

Leadership studies and organizational leadership models have progressed through three stages during the past fifty years. The first stage emphasized the behaviors and traits of superior or heroic leaders. The second stage focused on situational contingencies that affected the leadership behaviors displayed by supervisors. One of the more helpful tools from this period has been the Managerial Grid developed by Robert Blake and Jane Mouton, and later refined by Paul Hersey and Ken Blanchard into the Situational Leadership model that explores the balance between a leader's concern for people (relationships) and concern for production (tasks).

Hersey and Blanchard drew on principles from empirical research that found:

- leadership styles vary from leader to leader

- some leaders focus on initiating structure to accomplish tasks, others build and maintain relationships, some do both, and others do neither

- the most effective leaders adjust their behavior according to the situation

- the best style includes both high-task and high-relational orientation

- maturity in a follower's or team's job cycle must be treated similarly to parents with offspring who grow from novices to producers to experts

The third stage of leadership models, Leader-Member Exchange (LMX), focuses on the quality and quantity of the two-way interactions between a leader and follower. LMX theory "describes how a leader develops an exchange relationship over time with each subordinate as the two parties influence each other and negotiate the subordinate's role in the organization," notes Gary Yukl in *Leadership in Organizations*.

In an article for *The Leadership Quarterly*, George Graen and Mary Uhl-Bien surveyed a quarter century of development of the LMX theory and concluded that the strength of a dyadic, or 1-to-1, relationship depends upon increasing respect, trust, and mutual obligation between a leader and follower. Also, they observed, to the extent that a leader offers each follower more opportunity and responsibility over time, the leader-follower relationship will develop through definite stages: from stranger to acquaintance to an empowered mature partner. Partners ultimately become an "in-group." Graen and Uhl-Bien also noted:

> [that this transformation] to 'partnerships' is accompanied by a movement among members beyond their own self-interests to focus more on larger mutual interests. By satisfying 'partnership' interests, both members are also able to fulfill their own interests and more. When this occurs, formalized hierarchical relationships are no longer emphasized by the partners and the relationship becomes one more like peers than superior-subordinate.

I have personally experienced this shift from formal reporting relationship to peer relationship many, many times through my years as a field leader. For example, while living in Asia, Chris and his wife Amy were members of our team. They lived in the apartment one floor below us for four years. Their capacity for people and for leadership became obvious very early, so I gave away as much responsibility as I could to Chris. I even gave him my job as local team leader after six months so that I could focus more of my attention on developing leaders in four other cities. The close proximity of our lives provided daily opportunities for interaction, fun, and occasional conflict.

Four years later, when Ann and I moved to Singapore, Chris assumed my prior leadership role and still reported to me, though at a huge geographical distance. Our friendship helped close that distance. Chris was able to speak honestly to me, even in front of my other direct reports, when he felt my leadership compass was off by a few degrees. This helped create a less formal leadership culture where many hierarchy-conscious Asians could feel more like peers to me and to one another.

Teammates working in this type of positive environment with their leader consistently experience greater job satisfaction, lower turnover, more opportunities for advancement, and higher levels of personal initiative. In short, happy workers are productive workers. LMX theory has been criticized by some for seeming simplistic, and because the idea of an exclusive "in-group" runs counter to many societies' concept of fairness. However, it is widely recognized as one of the best predictors of leader-follower satisfaction and productivity because it prescribes relational behaviors that build trust, respect, and mutual obligation. Top-tier leaders consistently move from one-way to reciprocal relational influence, that is, they allow themselves to be influenced by their followers, as Steve allows the executive team to influence him, as much as they assume their role is to influence their followers. Table 3 summarizes the phases in relational leadership growth.

Table 3. Phases in Leadership Making

	Phase 1 STRANGER	Phase 2 ACQUAINTANCE	Phase 3 PARTNER
Roles	Scripted	Tested	Negotiated
Relational Influence	One way	Mixed	Reciprocal
Exchanges	Low quality	Medium quality	High quality
Interests	Self	Self and other	Group or Team
		TIME →	

Source: Adapted from Peter G. Northouse, *Leadership: Theory and Practice*, 4th ed. (Thousand Oaks, CA: Sage Publications, 2006), 156.

Transformational leadership was explored in books by James Burns and Bernard Bass as a move from transactional leadership models that focused on management by exception or contingent rewards toward change-oriented leadership. "Leadership, unlike naked power-wielding, is inseparable from followers' needs and goals," Burns stated in *Leadership*.

A transformational leader raises the self-consciousness of his or her followers to value outcomes, the means used to achieve them, and to transcend personal self-interest for the good of the team or organization. Transformational leaders use inspirational motivation, idealized influence (leading by example),

> *In short, happy workers are productive workers.*

intellectual stimulation, and individual consideration to achieve their goals.

Charismatic leadership shares many characteristics of transformational leadership, particularly idealized influence and inspirational motivation. But it differs in that "charismatic leadership typically instills both awe and submission in followers, whereas transformational leadership seeks to increase the engagement of followers," according to Richard Daft and Patricia Lane in *The Leadership Experience*.

While each of these earlier leadership models has merit, many of the studies from which they drew only observed leaders who had the luxury of close supervision over subordinates in their organization. As a result, they tend toward leader-centered models that do not directly address the challenges of distance and fluidity—at least not in the magnitude experienced by today's global managers.

Craig Pearce and Jay Conger explain in *Shared Leadership*:

> Although these models differ in important ways, they presume that the way in which we can enhance our understanding of leadership is to study patterns of employee supervision.... Organizations today feature more emphasis on efficiency and productivity, continuous innovation, decreased stability, more difficulty achieving and maintaining profitability, changed employment relations, and altered internal structures.... This pattern of evolution includes the emergence of network forms of organization.... Unlike hierarchical organizations, network organizations do not institutionalize structural authority that can ensure the resolution of conflicting interests.... Emerging organizational structures simply cannot

rely on the close supervision made possible by tall, hierarchical organizations.

If today's dynamic global realities render a close-proximity supervisory leadership style inadequate, how can leadership be defined? Yukl suggests that leadership is "the process of influencing others to understand and agree about what needs to be done and how to do it, and the process of facilitating individual and collective efforts to accomplish shared objectives." Leadership, then, becomes about defining appropriate work and seeing it accomplished; it does not focus on a single person or his or her position. Leadership is not limited to who has the authority to make a final decision, which is often what many practical discussions about leadership degenerate into. In daily reality, any follower in an organization can exert significant levels of shared leadership—even if he or she is not the formally appointed leader of a team, division, function, or distributed task force.

Defining leadership in this way helps free our minds from military (command and control) or industrial-age (production) models that have little to do with building high-trust relational networks of people extended across geographic or organizational boundaries. As Greenleaf is quoted in Dirk van Dierendonck and Kathleen Patterson's *Servant Leadership*, "The people are the institution!"

Servant leadership is a follower-centric model. It emphasizes "increased service to others, a holistic approach to work, building a sense of community, and the sharing of power in decision-making," says Larry Spears in *Focus on Leadership*. He cites ten attributes of servant leadership that highlight a leader's character: listening, empathy, healing, awareness, persuasion, conceptualization, foresight, stewardship, commitment, and community building. Patterson meanwhile lists seven virtues of servant leadership as *agapao* love, humility, altruism, vision, trust, empowerment, and service, the very qualities we observed in the apostle Paul's leadership. Servant leaders "lead with love, are motivated by love, and serve their followers with love," Dierendonck and Patterson conclude.

Servant leadership provides an ethical and moral foundation that both grounds and transcends previous leadership models. It is a logical extension of transformational leadership, which sought to empower the follower primarily to benefit the organization and its goals. In his leadership dissertation, Jeffrey Matteson differentiates between the two:

> In contrast with transformational leadership, servant leaders are less focused on the intellectual stimulation of followers and are more likely to take the emotional health of followers into account. Furthermore, servant leadership will produce a spiritually generative culture as opposed to the empowered dynamic culture of transformational leadership.

Leadership expert Jim Laub produced an instrument that measures the level of servant leadership present in organizations, the Organizational Leadership Assessment (OLA). In his view, the effective servant leader values people, develops people, builds community, displays authenticity, provides leadership, and shares leadership. In *Proceedings of the 2003 Servant Leadership Research Roundtable* he describes a servant organization as one in which "the characteristics of servant leadership are displayed through the organizational culture and are valued and practiced by the leadership and the workforce."

The OLA measures the progression of an organization from **autocratic** (leader as dictator, putting the needs of the leader first, treating others as servants) to **paternalistic** (leader as parent, putting the needs of the organization first, treating others as children) to

servant (putting the needs of those led first, treating others as partners).

People tend to hold one of two diametrically opposing views of leadership. One end of the spectrum is autocratic leadership, which stems from power, authority, and control.

> *Servant leadership is a follower-centric model.*

The other end is servant-based, which Laub defines as "the understanding and practice of leadership that places the good of those led over the self-interest of the leader."

Paternalism is the middle ground between the two extremes. From research involving more than eight hundred individuals in forty-one organizations, Laub found that most employees experience paternalistic leadership. Benevolent paternalistic leadership stems from a leader's self-view as parent over those being led, he observed, and "has the effect of producing a childlike response in the followers. The led readily accept that the leaders know more, are wiser and the led must simply follow, even if it means abdicating their own responsibility to lead."

This means that even benign paternalistic leadership does not pass Greenleaf's test of servant leadership ("Do those served grow as persons?"). Nor does it result in multiplying more mature leaders who view themselves as partners in their organization's mission. Paternalistic leadership exerted for too long stunts the development of followers. Ultimately, the strongest organizations don't parent their people; they raise and release mature servant leaders.

A few recent studies have looked at the relationships between servant leadership and distance leadership, or servant leadership and cross-cultural leadership. In one, William Shirey examined the effects of advanced communications technology on leader-follower relationships in the U.S. Department of Defense—finding that relationship quality was compromised by technology-related distractions in virtual communications. This comes as no surprise to anyone who has suffered being cut off during a Skype meeting. These distractions led to the perception of a lack of respect and commitment. In addition, busyness, workload, anxiety, and stress were contributing factors to increased psychological distance between leaders and followers.

Interviewing five high-profile Latin American leaders in Panama, Magda Serrano found that servant leadership qualities such as trustworthiness, loyalty, and development of others were seen as keys to effectiveness in that cultural context, while selfishness, negativity, lack of humility, lack of integrity, lack of education, and low empowerment were notable hindrances.

Power and its use are central to the discussion of servant leadership, argues James Showkeir. "*Persuasive power* creates opportunities and alternatives so individuals can choose and build autonomy," he writes in *Servant Leadership*. "*Coercive power* is used to get people to travel a predetermined path. The servant-leader practices persuasive power and walks a fine line in most people's minds." Showkeir concludes that in order for servant leaders to meet Greenleaf's test of developing others who are more autonomous and able to serve others, it is "essential to actively and intentionally distribute organizational power … [which] requires focusing attention on the culture, management practices, and architecture of the organization."

Servant leaders actively and intentionally distribute organizational power. Most leaders – in almost every culture – seek to assimilate and consolidate power. I have personally observed several situations, in our organization and in other Christian ministries, where the top positional leader became threatened by some of his talented senior leaders and had them fired or reassigned to other less influential roles. This behavior demotivates other followers and creates an environment where few leaders aspire to lead with that senior leader, either out of fear or knowing that they will not be able to use their strengths. One of my early mentors warned me to take care "not to allow the moon to shine brighter than the sun." Insecure leaders feel threatened when they hear that "Saul has slain his thousands, but David his ten thousands" (1 Samuel 18:7, 21:11, 29:5). Secure servant leaders pray for five more Davids to join their team.

MaryKate Morse endorses the need for top leaders to encourage frank talk about power within an organization. In *Making Room for Leadership*, she says:

> To be intentional about a group's use of power means to create a culture where power and influence are frequently discussed and evaluated…. The more diverse and complex the organizational structure of a group, the more difficult it is to bring cohesion around new goals and directions. Simply adding an assessment tool for an occasional check-up on the leader's and group's use of power is not enough. Power awareness can't be created with a program. It must be embedded in the culture.

I have observed that Christian leaders find it easy to talk about empowerment but shy away from talking directly about power— who has it, how it is distributed, and how well it is currently being used to advance the mission. Money, sex, and power are three temptations lurking in wait for every leader. We fire people in ministry for the misuse of money or sexual immorality. But when was the last time you heard of anyone who was removed from a position or even publicly confronted for abuse of power in the ministry? As leaders we must open up dialog about the positive and negative uses of power.

One way I have found to help bridge the power distance gap is to treat every leader I am responsible for as a peer. For years I have closed most of my emails with the phrase "Shoulder to shoulder" before my signature. Frequently people will comment on how those three words impact them. Think about that image. Side by side instead of over and under. It's powerful. It's one small but consistent message that signals "you're important and we're all in this together." I pray it helps flatten the organization by removing psychological distance.

In the face of immense distance and culture challenges, servant leadership goes beyond the former leader-focused leadership theories to a morally grounded follower-focused theory.

> *Servant leaders actively and intentionally distribute organizational power.*

Servant leadership provides the primary means to overcome power issues based on individual egos. Servant leaders lead with *agapao* love that seeks to do the right thing for the right reasons at the right time for the parties in question. Servant leadership rejects egocentric use of positional power to ensure compliance, and instead uses *personal and positional* power based on loving concern for those being led to ensure commitment. They have crucified the flesh and its drivenness to abuse the power inherent in an organizational position.

Was the man whom Erick Schenkel encountered truly a servant leader? Here is his conclusion, "As the discussion of servant leadership progressed, I was surprised to find that the acting leader, whose performance on this point I expected to hear questioned, was often referenced as an example of servant leadership. Finally, I asked one team member to explain why he saw this person as a servant leader. He told me that during the recent civil war in that country, this person has crossed the firing line regularly, risking his life to take food and heating fuel to villages cut off by the fighting. He shared how the leader had visited a women's prison, deprived of funding during the war and in terrible condition, and decided on the spot that his entire team would return and work there daily until they had created a livable environment for the prisoners. He told me that this leader had decided that he would never own his own home, and that he lived on the ministry property overseeing dozens of former orphans, former prisoners and young disciples.

"I realized that my criteria for servant leadership, based on an American checklist of expressions of servanthood, were leading me to miss the point. Servant leadership is not a set of practices, it is a heart of self-sacrificial passion. It is the driving motivation of a leader submitted to Christ, who came 'not to be served, but to serve...and to give His life as a ransom for many.'

"Yes, we did appoint the acting leader to lead the team—as if he needed our appointment—and through the years he has grown in some of the graces that we democratic westerners understand to be essential ways of communicating other-centeredness. But I thank God that He did not allow us to miss the most important thing—the man's heart."

"Jesus said, 'Woe to you Pharisees, because you give God a tenth of your mint, rue and all other kinds of garden herbs, but you neglect justice and the love of God. You should have practiced the latter without leaving the former undone'" (Luke 11:42).

Growing Close as a Servant

Field research among top global leaders surfaced these essential characteristics and competencies. An effective servant leader:

1. Fully embraces God's call to global level leadership of the organization

2. Increases in virtues of *agapao* love, humility, altruism, vision, trust, empowerment, and service

3. Listens in order to understand and empathize

4. Embraces suffering (pruning, pain, rejection, increased criticism, and misunderstanding)

5. Shares leadership; follows and leads equally well

The people we lead over distance cannot read our minds; they can only experience our behaviors and actions as we demonstrate them.

For Reflection and Action

- Which of these competencies do you currently practice well? If you asked some of the people you lead where you excel, what might they say?

- Which competency intrigues you as a place to grow next?

- Name two people who model that competency well; people of whom you would say "I'd love to learn from this person." How might you engage this person in helping you grow in this specific area?

- Did any specific book or article references catch your attention while reading through this chapter? Consider exploring those resources.

- Ask God for increasing self-awareness, growth, and fruitfulness.

Recommended Resources

The Leadership Challenge: How to Make Extraordinary Things Happen in Organizations by James M. Kouzes and Barry Posner, 5th Edition. If I could only recommend one book for changing your perspective on leadership and improving how you lead, it would be this one. Why? Because it highlights five common practices that model exemplary leadership in any culture. The practices are behaviors that you can learn, do, and teach others. The newly released 5th edition has over 100 all-new case studies, showing the practices in action around the world. It is based on 25 years of research among millions of leaders. Available in hard cover, Kindle, audio and with a workbook.

The Servant: A Simple Story about the True Essence of Leadership by James C. Hunter. There is a reason this book has sold over 3.5 million copies worldwide in the past 15 years. Highly recommended. Available in paperback or Kindle here. Note that there is a newly updated 2012 edition.

Upside Down: The Paradox of Servant Leadership by Stacy Rinehart. (Colorado Springs, CO: Navpress, 1998.) Available in paperback here.

7

CLOSE THE DISTANCE

He who does the work is not so profitably employed
as he who multiplies the doers. Count the day lost
that you do not do something, either directly or indirectly,
to multiply the number of unselfish workers.
- John R. Mott, longtime leader of the YMCA and Student
Volunteer Movement

Leading people is always challenging. Effective leadership that is satisfying for all involved requires ample personal contact. Distance of any kind can hinder these personal interactions, thwarting the necessary development of strangers into trusted partners. It is crucial for leaders operating in a complex global environment to recognize the unsleeping enemies of effective influence.

According to Barbara Napier and Gerald Ferris in their article "Distance in Organizations," leadership distance has three primary dimensions: psychological, structural, and functional. As a formula for failure in leader-follower relationships, it might be expressed like this:

Psychological distance + Structural distance = Functional distance

Some of the components contributing to a sense of distance between a leader and follower are summarized in Table 4.

Research typically focuses on one set of distance indicators while ignoring the others, falling short of offering a holistic approach to closing the distance leadership gaps in organizations. It's worth noting that distance factors can be found at any organizational level, too—from local to city to regional to global. For instance, a volunteer and supervisor in a local ministry community of two hundred people may experience as much or more functional distance—in terms of relationship satisfaction—as a globally distributed work team operating across four time zones.

Suzanne Weisband writes in *Leadership at a Distance: Research in Technologically-Supported Work* that friction can arise because "work is continuous and complex; people move from one task to another, and remote people are not typically a part of the day-to-day work that most people find themselves doing locally. Local managers tend to favor local employees and work." Younger, technologically savvy leaders who naturally contribute over distance may also put pressure on more traditional managers who have not adapted to the new rules of work and have trouble blending local and distance work. As any unhappily married couple can testify, physical proximity is no guarantee of relational satisfaction.

Table 4. Dimensions of Leadership Distance

Type of Distance	General Indicators	Specific Indicators
Psychological Distance	Demographic similarity	Age, sex, education, experience, race
	Power distance Perceived similarity Values similarity	Work values, sex roles, cultural values
Structural Distance	Design distance Opportunity to interact Spatial distance Span of management	Office design, physical distance Social contact at work, social contact outside work, accessibility, frequency
Functional Distance	Affect (emotional) Perceptual congruence Latitude Relationship Quality	Liking, Support, Trust Sex role perception Role discretion/ Autonomy Influence in decision-making Supervisor satisfaction, relationship satisfaction

Adapted from "Distance in Organizations" in *Human Resource Management Review 3* by Barbara J. Napier and Gerald R. Ferris

In organizations, however, the question arises: when does a conventional, localized team become a distributed, virtual team? Four decades of research by MIT professor Tom Allen indicate that geographic separation begins to significantly influence member-to-member interactions with distances as small as fifty feet, according to Jessica Lipnack and Jeffrey Stamps' *Virtual Teams: People Working Across Boundaries with Technology*. Once teammates are separated by more than 500 feet, a smooth working relationship may require the same level of intentionality as one 5,000 miles away. How many people are you currently leading that are located more than 500 feet away from you?

Many core business processes demand involvement from people working in different parts of the organization. For instance, recently I noticed that half of the senior staff members assigned to my team were also participating on at least one, if not two, global task forces or project teams. I was glad to share their talents with other leaders in our organization. When handled well, these stretch assignments develop the individuals while advancing our mission.

Rarely do all these people report to the same boss, yet these virtual teams are expected to deliver real work. Thus the notion of a "single boss" work environment does not fit the realities of a distributed work paradigm. In a multinational ministry environment, it is not uncommon for an employee to participate on two or more distributed teams or work groups simultaneously. Table 5 highlights the differences between conventional, virtual, and global teams.

Table 5. Differences Between Conventional, Virtual, and Global Teams

Type of Team	Spatial Distance	Communications	Member Cultures	Leader Challenge
Conventional	Localized	Face-to-face	Similar	*High*
Virtual	Scattered	Mediated	Similar or different	*Higher*
Global	Widely scattered	Mediated	Very different	***Very high***

Adapted from *The Leadership Experience*, 4th ed., by Richard L. Daft and Patricia Lane (Thomson/South-Western).

Comparing four extensive academic works on teamwork with two comprehensive and practical works on virtual teaming, I found that the effectiveness of a team—localized or virtual—depends upon five common elements. They are:

- a compelling team purpose or goal which is clear to all members

- trusting relationships

- communication which includes content, frequency, and agreed-upon processes

- task competence possessed by the members and the team leader

- timely achievement of desired results

The absence of any one of these elements will result in underperformance for both kinds of team.

Team Size

The size of any team affects relationships and effectiveness. Research on team size began more than thirty years ago when Ivan Steiner investigated what happened each time the size increased on a given team. He found that optimal team productivity peaked at about five members—a very small number. Adding members beyond five people decreased motivation, increased coordination problems, and resulted in a general decline in performance.

In *Cross-Functional Teams*, Glenn Parker suggests that depending on the mission, the optimal team size is four to six members, but a core team of five to eight members can effectively function as long as additional people are organized into an extended team or subgroups. As one experienced team leader explained to him, "Team effectiveness breaks down when you get beyond ten members... It was hopeless until we decided to have a core group of seven."

Other leadership experts have found that the development and display of shared leadership within teams is positively associated with proximity and negatively associated with team size. Examining extensive research, Pearce and Conger argued in *Shared Leadership* that team effectiveness, integration, and sustainability all decrease with increasing team size. Effective distance leaders will learn to break large teams of eight or more members into subteams, each with their own team or process leader.

The Trust Factor

"Just recently I had a short Skype conversation with one team member who told me that we were making a minor adjustment to a process that I had been leading," said Ruth McNeill, Cru's Western European Area director for Leadership Development and Human

Resources. She continued, "A second team member who had had a face-to-face conversation about the same topic informed me that it was actually a major change and one that I was not happy with. When I asked for the issue to be put in writing I found it was very different than what had been communicated verbally. I felt devalued and undermined. When I prayed about it, I realized that I had a choice to make. I could get angry and defend my point of view, or I could try to find out what was behind the change and see if there was a way to move forward. By now I've learned to choose the latter.

"While we use English as our common language, the fact that we are trying to communicate over distance, from different mother tongues, in different time zones, and with varying degrees of Internet connectivity adds stress to relatively small issues. Vain imaginations can run riot while you wait to read the next email installment.

"God has taught me to choose to believe the best and trust my team. I must fight to find out God's perspective rather than my own and to always seek the way forward."

Ruth is an excellent leader, but her experience demonstrates how virtual teams can amplify the normal problems most local teams face. For instance, Joseph Grenning wrote in *Leadership Excellence* how six hundred professionals who manage or work on virtual teams reported that common problems such as not following through on commitments, questioning team decisions, backbiting, and avoidance of conflict occur far more frequently on virtual teams.

Meanwhile, distributed virtual teaming supports the trend in institutions and organizations seeking to become more responsive to today's social media environment. In a *Harvard Business Review* blog, John Kotter highlighted the creative tension necessary for today's organization to maintain a good balance between hierarchy (whose strengths are standardization, stability, maintenance, and optimization) and network (whose strengths are seizing opportunity, rapid knowledge and expertise acquisition, and adaptability).

Whether teams are localized or virtual, trust is listed at or near the top of the list of team-building essentials in almost all literature. "Trust is the team members' reliance on one another to protect their joint endeavor," say Michael Marquardt and Lisa Horvath in *Global Teams*. Pat Lencioni also underscores the importance trust plays in *The Five Dysfunctions of a Team*:

> Trust lies at the heart of a functioning, cohesive team. Without it, teamwork is all but impossible... Trust is the confidence among team members that their peers' intentions are good, and that there is no reason to be protective or careful around the group. In essence, teammates must get comfortable being vulnerable with one another.

Nineteen of thirty chapters in *The Handbook of High Performance Virtual Teams* refer to the topic of trust. It is a key element of open leadership and decision-making, and can be greatly enhanced or destroyed through the proper use of social media, observes Charlene Li in *Open Leadership*.

Miheret Tilahun, the director of Digital Strategies for Cru in Southern and Eastern Africa, is an example of someone who built relationships and empowered workers through the use of social media in distance leadership. He explains, "I was the only assigned staff working on digital strategies at that time. God brought me a handful of students from three campuses that attended our first vision-casting program. Immediately I invited them to a closed Facebook group where we could share our ideas and connect. Over time we engaged in Facebook communication and a planned monthly Skype call as we were scattered throughout the country.

"In the first phase all of them formed digital strategies team on their three campuses. One campus, Hawassa University, now has a membership of more than twenty students. I visited these campuses to conduct trainings and gave some tools they can use for reaching their campus for Jesus.

"During the ongoing Skype conversations, we discussed our desire to expand our online ministry presence from three campuses into ten. The idea was well accepted by the three campuses that were on the Skype call. In the second phase, these four leaders from three campuses took the new challenge and expanded the ministry into ten campuses. It was exciting to see them doing it by themselves! They used all opportunities offline and online to help other universities to get onboard with online student ministries.

"Now as I am writing this we have 14 campuses from ten universities who are active in online ministries in Ethiopia. And students, not staff members, are leading all these initiatives. These local online ministry presences have produced an opportunity to conduct a series of national Facebook Evangelism Days online. I hear amazing testimonies from them. They are truly empowered to lead."

Miheret exemplifies many characteristics true of effective servant and distance leaders: trust, vision, empowerment, personal competence, and humility.

The lending and earning of trust is particularly crucial to distributed teams because it is the cornerstone of genuine collaboration. In *The Truth About Leadership*, James Kouzes and Barry Posner identify ten truths about leadership based on more than two million responses to their Leadership Practices Inventory from over seventy countries. "Credibility is the foundation of leadership" is the second truth; "Trust rules" is the sixth.

Tom Rath and Barry Conchie answer the question "What will people follow in organizational leaders?" in *Strengths-Based Leadership*. They offer four clear research-based responses: trust, compassion, stability, and hope. Most distributed teams lack face-to-face opportunities to develop trust in traditional ways, so they must develop "swift trust," which Marquardt and Horvath define as where each member "acts as if trust is present from the beginning."

We've built swift trust on two of the virtual teams I have led by talking about a relational trust bank. We all know how positive contributions and words of encouragement build up a positive bank account. Conversely, negative attitudes, criticism, and unfulfilled commitments decrease the trust account. When we launched a new virtual team, I asked everyone to pretend they were placing a $100 bill in the middle of the table as a down payment in the team's trust account. Then I explained, "The bumps and bruises that will naturally occur as we rub our ideas against each other will decrease our account, ten cents here, fifty cents there. But let's extend a lot of grace to one another. Let's start with a high balance of trust and not let the small things bring team momentum to a halt."

Communication

Excellent communication is non-negotiable for team success. "Twenty years ago, when I lived overseas, communication felt labored," explains Cheryl Boyd, Executive Director of Digital Strategies. "Now, it's easy to assume that it has occurred when, in fact, it has not. This is the challenge today. I don't take as much time laboring over what I am going to say and how I will be understood. I can launch a text message, voicemail, email, tweet, or blogpost and then assume that I was heard, understood, and that others are following me. The exciting challenge now is in crafting a message using the tools I have at my fingertips so that those I lead are blessed by receiving it."

Technology is both a blessing and a challenge when it comes to closing the distance in ministry. Used well, it can enhance and multiply our efforts. The key is to remain aware of the potential pitfalls, plan accordingly, and give plenty of grace. Erik Butz, Vice President of Global Operations, has clocked countless hours leading over a distance and gives these suggestions for communication:

"We all know that running an effective meeting is tough, even with a group from the same culture that is sitting in the same room. But even more things can trip you up when you're trying to lead a virtual meeting with people across multiple locations, time zones, languages and cultures.

"I've been a team member or leader of distributed teams for over a decade now. Although technology has been making it easier and easier for these teams to have virtual meetings, there are still many challenges - including the use of all the new technologies! The last few years, most of my time has been spent working with people over distance. I feel like I've been in the virtual meeting school of hard knocks during that time. The following is a list of best practices that I (Erik) have found helpful for holding fun and effective virtual meetings."

How To Lead Effective Virtual Meetings

1. **Establish a strong foundation of relationship and trust by having initial (and occasional ongoing) face-to-face meetings with your virtual team.** Solid relationship and trust are crucial to help overcome the inevitable miscommunications that happen over distance, emails and time (see Do you trust me?). If the team is a short-term work group, face-to-face

time might not be possible, but you can still do initial relationship building over a video call. Take time to have people share about themselves, their strengths, working style, passions, vision for the project, etc.

2. **Develop and follow virtual meeting norms.** All meeting norms that a face-to-face team would use will still apply, i.e. start and end on time, have an agenda, come prepared, etc. In addition, you might find it helpful to clarify some additional "virtual meeting norms." This could include practical things like having remote participants sit in a quiet room (i.e. not a loud coffee shop), be online five minutes early in case of IT issues, make eye contact with the camera, or raising your hand (on video, or virtually on a chat window) if you're having trouble breaking into the discussion.

3. **Involve all participants in virtual meetings**. If all participants have a specific role in the meeting, I find they will be more engaged overall. In addition to facilitating specific topics of discussion, participants could also be assigned a "meeting role," such as taking meeting notes, action point recorder, norms enforcer, or timekeeper. Related tip: The action point recorder can type action points directly into your online shared document and then everyone can review, clarify and confirm those action points (see Tip #4 below) at the end of the meeting.

4. **Keep priorities and action points visible to all and promote group accountability**. Leveraging shared document technology like Google docs can really help your team communicate and focus. We use a Google doc action point list that we add to and review at every meeting. Team members mark tasks complete or add progress updates in real time. We also have shared

planning documents and priority lists that everyone can easily reference as they do individual planning and work.

5. **Leverage collaboration tools to save discussion time**. We often think of virtual meetings as being less efficient as being face-to-face. However, in some cases, a team can gather information and "think together" more quickly using online tools. Try having everyone type his or her input or answer to a question into a chat window. The facilitator can review answers and follow up on key points or questions. The Google doc feature of having multiple people type into one document simultaneously is an extremely efficient way to quickly gather and refine ideas. Have everyone type in brainstorming ideas, answers to evaluation questions, or other small group or individual work that you want to compile, review and refine in real time.

6. **Test your meeting technology and tools.** My teams and others I've observed have wasted WAY too much time on IT issues at the start of meetings. These issues could have been worked out by just 2-3 people testing the technology in advance of the meeting. Starting a meeting with tech problems can easily put a wet blanket on the mood and make people feel like your meetings are a waste of time. Related tips: (1) Use a video solution if possible as I've found that being on video significantly increases engagement. (2) Have a backup connection method available for the meeting in case your primary method fails.

7. **Train your team on meeting technology and collaboration methods.** As you adopt new virtual meeting technology (like a new video conference system) or practices (like online document sharing or project management tools), make sure to train the

team on how to use these tools. If you don't, you might see engagement drop and frustrations rise.

8. **Adjust for language and cultural issues.** Many distributed teams will have people from different cultures and language backgrounds. Those realities must be taken into account for the team to truly be effective. The current team I lead operates bilingually, with some stronger in one language than the other. As a result, we take meeting notes in both languages simultaneously (thus we have two note takers – see Tip #3). That allows someone who gets lost to quickly read up in their mother tongue.

Global Leadership Competence

"Culture eats strategy for breakfast," as Peter Drucker is said to have observed, meaning that the most wonderfully planned strategies will fail if a company's culture does not support implementation. Someone who led effectively at a national level does not automatically possess the strength of character and breadth of competencies required for effective multinational or global leadership. That said, there is no single agreed-upon profile of a global leader or manager.

A global manager could be one of three types of specialists: a business (or strategy) manager, a country manager, or a function manager. Or he or she could be part of the smaller corps of general corporate leaders who manage the complex interactions of all three.

Additional corporate skill training does not address the root causes of underperformance or failure in these complex roles. "The single greatest cause of difficulties in global business transactions is not a lack of technical expertise, hard work or good intentions—it is a lack of 'people skills' for relating successfully with counterparts from other countries and cultures," observes Ernest Gundling in *Working Globesmart.* His research revealed that underlying cultural differences that are consistent and predictable typically cause cross-border friction.

A growing body of empirical research concurs with this assessment. Warren Bennis concludes that in global leadership there is a critical difference between business-crossings (the "whats") and culture-crossings (the "hows"). In *Developing Global Executives*, he states that "mastering the context of *business-crossing* pales in comparison to grasping the *cultural/human* aspects of leading in a global society. The latter requires One Big Thing and that is, *transformation of the self*."

Growing into effective distance leadership requires intentional personal change.

The five studies mentioned below provide a sampling of research-based competencies of effective multinational and global leaders. What common themes do you notice?

Morgan W. McCall and George P. Hollenbeck (*Developing Global Executives: The Lessons of International Experience*, Harvard Business School Press) interviewed 101 global leaders from 36 countries and discovered:

1. Open-minded and flexible in thought and tactics

2. Cultural interest and sensitivity

3. Able to deal with complexity

4. Resilient, resourceful, optimistic, and energetic

5. Honesty and integrity

6. Stable personal life

7. Value-added technical or business skills

Maxine A. Dalton, Chris Ernst, Jennifer Deal, and Jean Leslie (*Success for the New Global Manager: What You Need to Know to Work Across Distances, Countries, and Cultures*, Jossey-Bass) interviewed 211 global and local managers and found top managers possessed:

1. International business knowledge

2. Cultural adaptability

3. Perspective-taking

4. Ability to play the role of an innovator

5. Ability to manage action, people, and information across distance

Timothy R. Kayworth and Dorothy E. Leidner (*Journal of Management Information Systems*) observed 13 culturally diverse global teams. Effective global leaders:

1. Deal with paradox and complexity by performing multiple leadership roles simultaneously

2. Act in mentoring role with high degree of understanding and empathy

3. Able to assert authority without being overbearing or inflexible

4. Provide regular, detailed, prompt communication to peers

5. Able to articulate role relationships (responsibilities) among virtual team members

Marshall Goldsmith, Cathy Greenberg, Alastair Robertson, and Maya Hu-Chan (*Global Leadership: The Next Generation*, FT/Prentice Hall) interviewed 200 high potential leaders from 120 companies around the world. These leaders were able to:

1. Think globally

2. Appreciate cultural diversity

3. Develop technological savvy

4. Build partnerships and alliances

5. Share leadership

Ernest Gundling (*Working Globesmart: 12 People Skills for Doing Business across Borders,* Davies-Black Pub.) interviewed two-dozen experts who have worked with 30,000 business people in multicultural environments. They observed competency in three main areas, each with four specific skills:

Interpersonal

1. Establishing credibility

2. Giving and receiving feedback

3. Obtaining information

4. Evaluating people

Group

5. Building global teamwork

6. Training and development

7. Selling

8. Negotiating

Organizational

9. Strategic planning

10. Transferring knowledge

11. Innovating

12. Managing change

The big idea here is: *Global leaders require a significantly higher level of personal capacity than similar domestic leadership roles.* Each global leadership role is unique, but common themes arising from empirical research demonstrate needs for increased personal credibility, humility, teachability, empathy (manifested as a desire to understand others), emotional stability, mutuality, stamina, ability to give and receive feedback, respect for cultural diversity, technological savvy, core business knowledge, solid management and communication skills, willingness to share leadership, and intellectual flexibility. Yes, the list can be daunting, but if you look closely you will see a lot of similarity with the nine fruits of the Spirit described in Galatians 5:22-23. God is committed to growing his leaders in both character and competence.

For distance leaders, building and sustaining trusting relationships with subordinates, partners, peers, and other leaders must be accomplished quickly through multiple means of telecommunications technology. Many of these essential qualities reflect the heart-level transformation needed by those who would aspire to lead as servants first.

Timely Achievement of Desired Results

Talk is cheap. As one of my friends says, ultimately all good meetings must degenerate into action.

As a global servant, you can develop great relationships. You can master the technology. But if your distributed team can't deliver real work on time and on budget, you're not getting the job done.

Some of us lean more naturally toward execution. Others need more help. I have tried many tools. Here's what I am currently using to help me and my distributed teams execute action across distance:

1.   Have a personal workflow framework. I highly recommend "Getting Things Done" by David Allen.

2.   Have one place to take notes on every significant conversation. For years I struggled to have one "place" to record all my conversations with various leaders. I had some notes in my journal, others in a notebook, others typed into a Word doc on my computer, and rarely

the right ones with me when I needed them. But technology has now enabled me to recall the notes I need, when I need them, no matter where I am. Rather than having a complex file system, I just need my notes to be searchable. And they must be portable because many of my conversations happen away from my office, when I only have my smartphone or tablet with me. The tool must work across multiple devices (phone, tablet, computer). I have found Evernote to be the best tool for this purpose.

3. Use a Task/To Do list. You're smart, but your memory is not reliable enough to handle the speed and complexity of your role. My task list must work across multiple devices (phone, tablet, computer). I will keep temporary to-do notes in a written journal but I transfer them to one common list as soon as possible.

4. Nurture a balanced lifestyle that allows you to travel well. It's important to maintain a healthy perspective on travel as a necessary part of distance leadership. I wrote the following blog post to share my thoughts.

On Traveling Well

For the past 18 years, Ann and I have been blessed to serve in distance leadership roles within our global movement. I have traveled about 90 nights per year for the past decade. During this season of our ministry we have raised two children, lived in three countries, and visited every continent except Antarctica.

Here are a few of the lessons God has taught us on traveling well:

• **Gratefully embrace God's call.** The Spirit is always at work. Habakkuk 1:5 says, "Look among the nations! Observe! Be astonished! Wonder!" Being involved with Campus Crusade allows us to see God at work in unique and incredible ways. When I feel pressured by hectic schedules, jet lag, and extended time on the road, it's good to remember that God has called us to deeply significant work with incredible people around the world.

• **It's more about rhythm than balance.** Balance implies that I need to keep all the plates spinning all the time. Trips don't always come in evenly-spaced, manageable patterns. Most of my travel is based on the needs and best timing for our field staff. This is part of serving them well—to be on their schedule and agenda. When I have an intense season of travel (more than eight days away in a month), I try to ensure that I have equally intense time at home and time to be with the teams I'm on. About ten years ago I made a commitment to take a weekly Sabbath — 24 hours away from email and thinking about work. A Sabbath is more than a day off – it's a day with people and pursuits that refresh me. God has used this single decision to consistently restore my heart and renew my strength.

• **Learn to discern.** Being asked to speak or travel can boost my ego. But every trip costs more than just money. I keep a running list of all current travel opportunities and I check with Ann and someone on my team before saying "yes." I ask: Do I (or we) really need to make this trip, Lord? If so, why? I created a simple worksheet in Excel to help me plan and track the number of nights away each year. I don't want to write checks that my body and my marriage can't cash.

• **(Pre-trip) Prepare everyone well.** When our children were younger we would open a map during dinner and talk about where daddy was going and which of their friends I might see, then pray together. Often I would carry notes and gifts to friends. This helped build a sense of being in the ministry together. I also try to get sufficient information about where I'm going and make sure to clarify expectations with those I will be visiting about what our agenda will look like. Otherwise, I risk unpleasant surprises or suboptimal use of their time.

• **(During trip) Be fully present.** Enjoy being attentive to God and people in the moment. That is why I'm here, right? If I'm stressing out about unanswered emails, other meetings, or problems elsewhere I am probably not engaging sufficiently. My distractedness communicates lack of personal concern.

• **(Post-trip) Follow through.** What did I commit to during my trip? To pray for someone? To make network connections? Other actions? If I can't follow through immediately, I make sure to capture my commitments in one of three places: Evernote, my mobile to-do list app, or in the top right corner of any handouts. On the plane or during my next planning time, I can review all my action points and follow through appropriately. Doing what I said I would do is one of the most important ways to build relationships of trust that can handle the strains of distance leadership.

Being aware of the challenges of frequent travel and proactively addressing them can help limit the stress you experience as you live out your calling and ministry responsibilities. May you go with God and travel well!

Growing in Closing the Distance

Field research among top global leaders surfaced these essential characteristics and competencies. An effective distance leader:

1. Leads a stable personal life

2. Leverages face-to-face and mediated communication to rapidly build trusting relationships

3. Asserts authority without being overbearing, inflexible, or controlling; mentors with empathy

4. Thinks globally; is able to solve increasingly complex problems and offer flexibility in local implementation

5. Builds virtual teams that connect people, manage information, and execute action across borders

For Reflection and Action

- Which of these competencies do you currently practice well? If you asked some of the people you lead which areas you excel in, what might they say?

- Which competency intrigues you as a place to grow next?

- Name two people who model that competency well; people of whom you would say "I'd love to learn from this person." How might you engage this person in helping you grow in this specific area?

- Did any specific book or article references catch your attention while reading through this chapter? Consider exploring those resources.

- Ask God for increasing self-awareness, growth, and fruitfulness.

Recommended Resources

Getting Things Done: The Art of Stress Free Productivity by David Allen. You need a clear workflow system to be an effective distance leader. This book has helped me grow in focus, prioritization, sequencing, and execution. Allen provides a helpful framework for managing personal workflow, multiple inboxes, tasks, and projects with one purpose: to get the most important work done. For the past ten years I have required each of my executive assistants to read this during their first week on the job. It's a flexible approach that can be adapted to a variety tools whether you use paper, computer, or smartphone apps. Available in paperback or Kindle here.

Ken's Blog, http://www.onleadingwell.com. I wrote a series of posts highlighting practical tips for leading virtual teams. You can find them by searching for "improve your virtual team" on my blog, or you can use this link.

8

GO CLOSE-CULTURAL

When it comes to getting things done, culture matters more than you think.

Cross-cultural misunderstandings aren't limited to when East meets West or North meets South. They can occur even in the same part of the world, where the possibility of insensitivity may be over-looked, as my friend Tariku Fufa discovered to his dismay.

Recently having been appointed to oversee student-led ministries in twenty-four countries in southern and eastern Africa, he convened a meeting of the various leaders in Addis Ababa, Ethiopia, where he had seen great success while heading student-led works there. The results of a regional survey he had commissioned had disappointed him, and he spoke strongly when sharing the findings with the assembled leaders.

"God is willing to do big things but you are limiting him," he said passionately, hoping to inspire his audience to faith and action. Instead, tension filled the room with some attendees speaking angrily, and worse still, the senior leader to whom Tariku reported saying that he disagreed with what Tariku had shared.

Surprised and saddened, Tariku spent the evening in prayer and reflection, and talked with his leader. The next morning as the meeting reconvened, he told the leaders he was sorry. He had been unwise in the way he spoke, he admitted, and had not taken into account the different circumstances that had been part of the reason for the greater results he had seen in Ethiopia.

"I immediately repented before the Lord and asked for forgiveness," Tariku told me. "I also resolved to listen more to what these leaders were saying." Tariku's acknowledgment of his blind spots was a turning point. The leaders to whom he apologized thanked him for his example of humility, "and as a result, we were able to build trust among ourselves." That openness in turn led to a breakthrough in discussions that produced an action plan that saw the student-led works concerned multiply from just over a hundred campuses to almost six hundred in the past two years.

The actions Tariku took – publicly admitting his own sin, asking for forgiveness from those he led, and resolving to listen – are not considered normal in his southern and east African culture. He had stumbled on to a key principle: in order to lead effectively across multiple national cultures, Tariku first had to overcome his own personal biases.

Everyone has cultural biases. These tendencies are consistent and well documented. There has been an explosion of cross-cultural and multinational research published in the past fifty years. Oft-cited studies include E.T. Hall's findings in *Beyond Culture* that a primary dimension of cultures is the degree to which they are individualistic or collectivistic. Hall also divided cultures based on high-context and low-context communication patterns.

High context cultures rely heavily on non-verbal nuances and the surrounding environment for accurate interpretation. They are concrete, paying attention to body language, tone of voice, and what else is going on in the room. Much of the global south and east are high context cultures. My Latin, African, Arab, and Asian colleagues refer to themselves as "highly relational" because they prefer to discuss important business face-to-face rather than over email.

Low context cultures, such as much of the global north and west, are more comfortable with abstract ideas, concepts, and principles. They are more concerned with the right wording rather than the speaker's tone of voice. They find their work goes smoother if key information is written down and communicated in the form of email, graphs, diagrams, or clear strategic plans. Opposing points of view or clarifying questions are often stated with unsettling directness. My European and North American colleagues refer to themselves as "highly relational" because they can use our limited face-to-face time to enjoy an espresso together. Work stuff has already been directly addressed and left behind at the office.

Every culture tends to view itself as highly relational. The difference is in how individuals in that culture prefer to relate.

Dutch culturist Fons Trompenaars surveyed more than fifteen thousand respondents from forty-seven nations and found that cultures could effectively be classified in two dimensions: egalitarian versus hierarchical, and person versus task orientation. Another Dutchman, professor Geert Hofstede, conducted a broader study beginning in 1968. Research gathered from 116,000 IBM middle managers in seventy-two countries led him to two significant conclusions pertaining to organizational culture. First, there are no universal, easily exportable solutions to organization and management problems. Second, "organizations are symbolic entities; they function according to implicit models in the minds of their members, and these model as culturally determined." In *Culture's Consequences* he commented:

> The survival of mankind will depend to a large extent on the ability of people who think differently to act together. International collaboration presupposes some understanding of where others' thinking differs from ours. Exploring the way in which nationality predisposes our thinking is therefore not an intellectual luxury.

Critics have argued that, though large, Hofstede's sample size was too narrow to draw solid conclusions from because of its focus on the middle managers of just one organization. However, research in social science continues to validate the distinguishable characteristics of culture across societies and their levels that he identified. Anthropologists, sociologists, and missiologists frequently refer to five dimensions, or indices, of culture and their shorthand initials, which Hosfstede proposed as a result of his study. They are:

- Power Distance (PDI)
- Uncertainty Avoidance (UAI)
- Individualism vs. Collectivism (IDV)
- Masculinity vs. Femininity (MAS)
- Long-term vs. Short-term Orientation (LTO)

These measures of culture allow any country or society to be positioned somewhere between their poles. These dimensions are not binary; they are more like sliding scales representing the degree to which a culture manifests this attribute. For example, though the

USA ranks 91 on the IDV index, it would not be accurate to say that the USA is a purely individualistic culture. The USA is a huge, diverse country with a number of clearly identifiable sub-cultures such as Hispanics, African-Americans, Asian-Americans, urban hipsters, Silicon Valley entrepreneurs, and so on. Some of those sub-cultures are more collectivistic. However, it would be accurate to expect many more individualistic tendencies in the USA than Thailand, which has an IDV index of 20.

If you're interested in learning how these five indices compare from nation to nation, there is an application in Apple's iTunes store called CultureGPS Lite that is designed to help distance leaders avoid cultural miscues by comparing two national cultures using Hofstede's five indices. The free app contains definitions and examples of each of the indices.

Hofstede's important work has been furthered in the GLOBE study, which is the shortened name of the Global Leadership and Organizational Behavior Effectiveness research project. Conceived and launched by Robert J. House in 1991, it spans more than a decade of research by a worldwide network of over a hundred and seventy social scientists working in sixty-two nations. Researchers surveyed more than seventeen thousand middle managers working for almost a thousand different companies in the food processing, financial services, and telecommunications industries to discern the relationships between behaviors and values.

For GLOBE, culture is defined as "shared motives, values, beliefs, identities, and interpretations or meanings of significant events that result from

Every culture tends to view itself as highly relational. The difference is in how individuals in that culture prefer to relate.

common experiences of members of collectives that are transmitted across generations."

Four cultural dimensions, or indices, identified by GLOBE that overlap with Hofstede's work are power distance, uncertainty avoidance, in-group collectivism, and institutional collectivism vs. individualism. GLOBE expanded upon Hofstede's work to add five more cultural dimensions, for a total of nine.

Figure 1 shows country clusters sharing similar cultures according to the GLOBE research.

I have found that the indices that consistently help predict and identify cross-cultural stress points are a blend of Hall's and Hofstede's work. I frequently do a quick evaluation on a culture I'm entering based on the following indices:

- High vs. Low Context

- High vs. Low Power Distance

- Individualistic vs. Collectivistic

- Uncertainty Avoidance vs. Comfort with Ambiguity

- Present vs. Future Orientation

These five are relatively easy to keep in mind and help me adjust on the spot in conversations or virtual meetings. For instance, someone from a culture high in power distance, context, and uncertainty avoidance will want to know who is in charge, prefer face-to-face interaction with their leader, and desire very clear expectations for their job. This may be challenging if their project or team leader comes from a more egalitarian culture that is low in those three areas.

Figure 1. Country Clusters
According to GLOBE Study

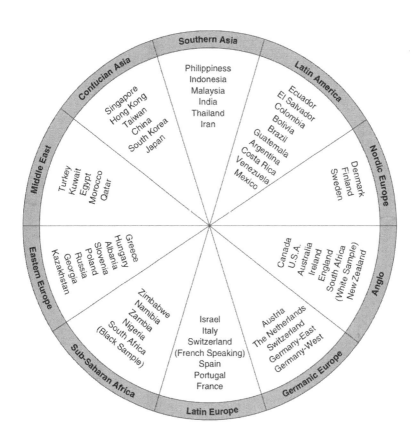

Source: Adapted from House *et al.*, *Culture, Leadership, and Organizations: The GLOBE Study of 62 Societies* (Thousand Oaks, CA: Sage, 2004), 190. Cultural similarity is greatest for societies within a cluster. Proximity on the diagram represents greater similarity in societal culture. For example, the Latin Europe cluster is most similar to Sub-Saharan Africa and least similar to Southern Asia.

The most user-friendly explanation I've found for how culture shapes leadership is in the book *Leading Across Cultures: Effective Ministry and Mission in the Global Church* by my friend Jim Plueddemann. I have included it as a recommended resource at the end of this chapter.

The brilliance of the GLOBE study may rest in its exploration of universally preferred leadership styles. GLOBE researchers sought to fill what is described in *Culture, Leadership, and Organizations: The Globe Study of 62 Societies* as "a substantial knowledge gap concerning cross-cultural forces relevant to effective leadership and organizational practices."

As there are no universally accepted definitions among social scientists of "leadership" or "culture," GLOBE developed the following working definitions:

> **Organizational leadership** is the ability of an individual to influence, motivate, and enable others to contribute toward the effectiveness and success of the organizations of which they are members.

> **Culture** is shared motives, values, beliefs, identities and interpretations or meanings of significant events that result from common experiences of members of collectives and are transmitted across age generations.

Researchers sought to answer questions such as: What are the desired behaviors, attributes, and organization of effective leadership that are universal across cultures? Are there specific leadership styles that hinder effectiveness? Which leadership styles are culturally contingent?

The project found that leadership effectiveness is contextual. Over and over again, the study quotes CEOs, managing directors, and global partners who acknowledge the severe shortage of culturally self-aware leaders capable of leading well across cultures. The official report notes:

> [The making of global managers] is easier said than done. Managers who work in the international arena are steeped in their own culture. They have lived many years of their lives in their own countries, have been educated there, and have spent years working there. It is not easy for one to understand and accept practices and values that vary from one's own personal experiences.

Supporting this from separate research, Richard Lewis states the issue more concretely in *When Cultures Collide: Leading Across Cultures*:

> Leaders cannot readily be transferred from culture to culture. Japanese prime ministers would be largely ineffective in the United States; American politicians would fare badly in most Arab countries; mullahs would not be tolerated in Norway. Cross-national transfers are becoming increasingly common with the globalization of business, so it becomes even more imperative that the composition of international teams, and particularly the choice of their leaders, be carefully considered. Autocratic French managers have to tread warily in consensus-minded Japan and Sweden. Courteous Asian leaders have to adopt a more vigorous style in argumentative Holland and theatrical Spain if they wish to hold the stage. German managers sent to Australia are somewhat

alarmed at the irreverence of their staff and their apparent lack of respect for authority.

In *Leadership in a Diverse and Multicultural Environment*, Mary
Connerley and Paul Pedersen told how they found that "multinational
companies do not and cannot submerge the individuality of different cultures, since the template for behaviors isn't from the company
but from the national culture," and noted that nationality exerted
three times more influence on leadership assumptions than any other
demographic.

Paul Borthwick, noting the need to affirm ethnicity while combating ethnocentricity, observed in his dissertation, "Increased asser-
tion of ethnic/cultural identity today within nations across the world
puts Christian leadership in some very tough places, trying to identify
with their own people but also trying to mediate peace, reconciliation,
and the biblical ideals of unity."

Should we conclude, then, that cross-cultural leadership is too
difficult to be successful? Returning to the GLOBE study, we find
that there are common qualities among top leaders which transcend
culture. The seventeen thousand respondents were also asked to rank
112 leadership behaviors and attributes on a scale of one (lowest;
greatly impedes outstanding leadership) to seven (highest; greatly con-
tributes to a person being an outstanding leader). These 112 attributes
generated twenty-one leadership scales, which were then grouped in
six global leadership dimensions, with varying numbers of associated
characteristics.

In summary, the GLOBE study recognizes the following as universally endorsed behaviors for effective leadership:

1. Being trustworthy, just and honest (integrity)

2. Having foresight and planning ahead (charismatic-visionary)

3. Being positive, dynamic, encouraging, motivating, and building confidence (charismatic-inspirational)

4. Being communicative, informed, a coordinator and team integrator (team builder)

The GLOBE team report distilled it this way: "The portrait of a leader who is universally viewed as effective is clear: The person should possess the highest levels of integrity and engage in Charismatic/ Value-based behaviors while building effective teams."

Conversely, the GLOBE team also reported eight universal characteristics that respondents listed as *inhibitors* of effective leadership. From the 62 national societies surveyed, no culture prefers to follow a leader who is a loner, asocial, noncooperative, irritable, non-explicit, egocentric, ruthless, or dictatorial. Go figure.

The GLOBE profile of an effective leader meshes well with extensive worldwide research on the characteristics of exemplary leaders over the past twenty-five years. Writing in *The Leadership Challenge*, James Kouzes and Barry Posner define an exemplary leader simply as "someone whose direction you would be willing to follow." They found that from a list of twenty leadership characteristics, *four have been consistently ranked at the top across different countries.* These four universally desirable leadership descriptors, in order, are:

1. Honest

2. Forward-looking

3. Inspiring

4. Competent

The research is very consistent. Good leaders can lead well across cultures because the most highly desirable leadership qualities are universal – and biblical. This list is strikingly similar to the leadership qualities demonstrated by the apostle Paul.

Yet culture still matters. Research clearly indicates that the national culture of one's upbringing plays a disproportionately significant role, up to three times more influential, in forming the assumptions a leader holds about his or her own leadership. This implicit mindset affects a leader's willingness to follow and be influenced by others. We must be able to identify our own cultural biases.

Any global leader seeking long-term effectiveness will learn how to manage cultural diversity by studying, respecting, and explicitly dealing with differences such as high and low power-distance cultures, high and low context cultures, individualistic and collectivist cultures, and so forth. James Plueddemann synthesizes these ideas well:

> For God's people to work together effectively, implicit assumptions about leadership need to be made explicit. They must be evaluated in light of sound social science research and biblical principles. The church in the North and South, the East and West acts out of unconscious and often confusing assumptions about leadership. We must appreciate the differences and challenge some of the misconceptions in order to work together as the worldwide body of Christ.

My conversations with many leaders in our organization supported much of the current research. Field leaders confirmed that while each culture has its own culturally contingent leadership characteristics, there are universally desirable and undesirable leadership characteristics that resonate in any cultures.

Fewer than half of the group of twenty senior leaders I interviewed had received cross-cultural training of any type. Eight had completed one of our organization's formal cross-cultural training courses, though only one of those leaders was non-American. The majority of non-American global leaders had little or no access to cross-cultural training. However, everyone who received cross-cultural training viewed it as helpful, regardless of the format. One leader observed:

> "No matter where I go I will never have a native cultural understanding of the second culture. So the foundation for me is a humble acknowledgment that I will never fully get it, which forces me to constantly be asking myself the question, 'How am I not getting it right now?' We learn by listening, watching, even if we don't ever fully understand the second culture. The whole idea of reverse mentoring, of realizing that even though we come as the person who is the teacher, who's on a mission to bring truth, that we need mentors who teach us the culture as well as the language. We must exercise the patience that comes with language learning and the cultural learning that's part of our cross-cultural training and the way we approach ministry in the early stages."

Another leader emphasized the need to explicitly acknowledge one's own cultural biases:

> "You have to recognize your own ethnocentricity. We all have a tendency to believe that our way is better than everyone else's way. I try to observe and understand what their culture is like and what communicates love and respect to them. Like with

the Latins—trying, even imperfectly, to speak their language."

A third spoke passionately about the difference between procla-mation and incarnation ministries, specifically mentioning Paul as an excellent model of cross-cultural proclamation who never sought to become a local elder. He observed, "What we do well is proclaim and find bridge people who we can disciple and pour our lives into who are going to get that local culture better than we could ever get it. We haven't always understood well our limitations as cross-cultural ministers."

Several of those I spoke with at length mentioned a common form of resistance they encountered in their interactions with other leaders. This resistance frequently came in the form of statements such as, "You don't understand my culture," or "Yes, that may work in your country, but we're different, it won't work here." Statements like this undermine trust and shut down further discussion. If left unaddressed by leaders, the underlying attitudes can create an ingrown, prideful organizational culture that fails to partner well or learn from others.

One leader who has spent years living and working cross-cultur-ally described the effect of these kinds of comments:

> "It freezes the conversation. You can no longer talk
> about strategy or spiritual things because everything
> is now, 'You don't get it.' I finally learned to call it
> that. I'd say, 'In my country, we have this expres-
> sion about playing a trump card, and that just stops
> the conversation. My encouragement to you is not to
> play the trump card so we can keep going and work
> through the issues. Our goal is to get past what I don't

understand or what you don't understand so we can get to the strategy of what God has called us to do.' I found that helpful—to help people realize that you really don't want to play that card."

Often a leader who possesses a limited or closed perspective will eventually be challenged to a leadership role involving a scope of many nations and cultures. It may take years of cultural mistakes and bruised relationships for that leader to learn to value each culture and extend freedom of expression to leaders, while calling them to unity in pursuing an agreed-upon global direction—if he ever learns the lessons at all.

All cultures are relational; God designed people to interact. Cultures simply express their relational-ness in different ways. God's love for every nation invites—even requires—Christians who regularly lead across cultural boundaries to take cross-cultural fluency seriously. It is a challenging but not impossible task, as Morgan McCall and George Hollenbeck note in Developing Global Leaders: The Lessons of International Experience:

> The systematic development of global leaders requires an even stronger, more focused environment than does a domestic effort…. Learning how to adapt to different cultures turns out to be both more important and more difficult than acquiring the business lessons…. Learning to work across cultures is an essential competency of the global executive, and it is for most people an emotional education as well as an intellectual one. In other words, the lessons are … often profoundly personal.

An important lesson in cross-cultural closeness comes from Andrea Buczynski, Vice President of Global Leadership Development and Human Resources for Cru. She shares the following story.

"Andrea, you cannot disengage."

I shrugged my shoulders and said, "I'm tired of knocking my head up against the wall. He is not going to change his opinion."

"If you don't engage, he will think that you do not care about the topic or his opinion."

He got my attention. This working relationship had been challenging. How could he think I didn't care about this topic - my passion? Feeling misunderstood and frustrated, I walked away rather than argue. But this friend raised an important point. I assumed that my style was better than my colleague's style.

My biggest lesson both in distance and cross-cultural leadership has been this: "don't assume anything."

Don't assume…

- the way you engage is the way others like to engage.

- words or behaviors are aimed at you personally. We can be at odds with one another right away if cultural styles are deemed personal affronts.

- your points of view are the same. Each of us has a unique vantage point even in common experience.

- events, situations, or emotions that others describe occur in the same way that you experience them. Common language can go a long way, but only if there is a common understanding behind it.

- people should trust you. You inherit whatever trust level previous leaders have had, good or bad. That is your starting point. Whether or not it continues depends on you.

- you understand the reasons for or causes of behavior or systemic problems without investigation. It is too easy to make assumptions without really understanding what's actually going on.

Philippians 2:4 says to not look on your own interests only, but look to the interests of others. So even though I felt uncomfortable, I went back to my colleague and pressed into the argument. Fewer than ten minutes later, we had an understanding. I assumed he was immoveable when he only wanted to test the reasoning.

My lesson is this: Don't assume. Take the time to understand the perspective of those you serve. Adjust your style to love and serve others well.

Growing Close-Culturally

Field research among top global leaders surfaced these essential characteristics and competencies. An effective cross-cultural leader:

1. Grows in self-awareness of personal cultural values and biases

2. Demonstrates cultural interest, sensitivity, and adaptability

3. Fosters mutuality and participation in all leadership venues

4. Understands cultural indices' impact on strategy implementation and adjusts leadership appropriately

For Reflection and Action

- Which of these competencies do you currently practice well? If you asked some of the people you lead which skills you excel in, what might they say?

- Where do you feel a need to grow next?

- Name two people who model that competency well; people of whom you would say "I'd love to learn from this person." How might you engage this person in helping you grow in this specific area?

- Did any specific book or article references catch your attention while reading through this chapter? Consider exploring those resources.

- Ask God for increasing self-awareness, growth, and fruitfulness.

Recommended Resources

Leading across Cultures: Effective Ministry and Mission in the Global Church by James C. Plueddemann. (Downers Grove, IL: IVP Academic, 2009.)

If you only have time to read one book on leading cross-culturally, this is the one. It is available in print and for Kindle here. Dr. Plueddemann speaks from a lifetime of experience in the mission field (Nigeria) and as a professor and chair of the mission and evangelism department at Trinity Evangelical Divinity School.

9

MOVE CLOSER

If you know these things, blessed are you if you do them.
Jesus to his disciples in John 13:17

At its essence, quality leadership continues to reflect this
two thousand year-old principle: Leading well is loving well.

Having considered the sweep of the biblical narrative and volumes of academic research, we return to the question that prompted my studies: if a global leader has no more than five days per year of face-to-face time with his or her co-laborers in a multinational context, how can that leader appropriately serve, strengthen, inspire, align, equip, and coach those field leaders to live and lead well throughout the other 360 days?

I believe that effective global leaders of the twenty-first century bear character qualities similar to first-century servant leaders as exemplified by Paul. Servant leaders are not wimps! Rather, they possess a paradoxical blend of virtues: love and vision, boldness and humility, zeal and patience, focus and inclusion, commitment and compassion.

They are passionate about God's purposes and God's people. They embrace suffering as a normal part of participating in God's mission. They eagerly share leadership; they can follow and lead equally well. Because close supervision is impossible, they employ a variety of methods, including advanced telecommunications technology, to build trusting relationships over distance. They are respectfully aware of the effects different national and organizational sub-cultures have on themselves and on their ability to lead others well.

Recommendations for Those Who Want to Lead Close

Close suggests a new paradigm for twenty-first century global leaders, which aims to add to and integrate, rather than replace, existing leadership paradigms. For organizations and individuals wanting to pursue this further, I recommend the following:

Lead well by loving well.

Servant leadership is typified first and foremost by a leader's genuine concern for his or her followers' well-being, evidenced by placing the followers' interests before one's own interests. The ministry of Paul provides a great example of this type of leadership.

Foster interest and create space for dialogue.

Articulate the distance leadership challenge, and affirm leaders who serve in that capacity. Top leaders must model personal commitment to a paradigm of servant leadership, distance leadership and cross-cultural leadership that adapts to local conditions while implementing global standards.

A New Paradigm for Leading Close

Aspect	Essential Characteristics and Competencies
Servant leadership	1. Fully embraces God's call to global level leadership of the organization 2. Increases in virtues of *agapao* love, humility, altruism, vision, trust, empowerment, and service 3. Listens in order to understand and empathize 4. Embraces suffering (pruning, pain, rejection, increased criticism, and misunderstanding) 5. Shares leadership; follows and leads equally well
Distance leadership	1. Leads a stable personal life 2. Able to leverage face-to-face and mediated communication to rapidly build trusting relationships 3. Able to assert authority without being overbearing, inflexible, or controlling; mentors with empathy 4. Global thinker; able to solve increasingly complex problems and offer flexibility in local implementation 5. Able to build virtual teams that connect people, manage information, and execute action across borders

Cross-cultural leadership	1. Grows in self-awareness of personal cultural values and biases
	2. Demonstrates cultural interest, sensitivity, and adaptability
	3. Fosters mutuality and participation in all leadership venues
	4. Understands cultural indices' impact on strategy implementation and adjusts leadership appropriately

Offer concise biblical examples.

Point people to models of servant leadership across distance and culture, such as Paul's approach to team ministry with Silas and Timothy in Thessalonica (Acts 17:1-9). As mentioned in chapter four, their first letter to the church at Thessalonica exemplifies team-based ministry focused on hope in Jesus Christ.

Use participatory action learning/research processes.

This will help global leaders increase their level of cultural self-awareness. Mutuality and participation are critical. In *Leadership in a Diverse and Multicultural Environment: Developing Awareness, Knowledge, and Skills*, Mary Connerley and Paul Pedersen advise, "Many have shared the frustration with the competency list phenomenon and feel that there must be more to multicultural leadership than a list of competencies.... The best development strategy may simply be to teach people the basics and help them 'learn how to learn.'"

Review your organization's leadership framework.

Consider or request a wide-ranging organizational review to solicit feedback on attitudes and behaviors related to servant leadership, effective use of advanced communications technology, and cross-cultural awareness.

Develop a list of resources.

Find books, articles, research and other materials specifically tailored for global leaders—and make it readily available online.

Offer or require short- and mid-term cross-cultural leadership opportunities.

These should be available at the global level; a common practice in multinational corporations but less frequent in mission agencies due to the perception of prohibitive costs. As Morgan McCall and George Hollenbeck note in *Developing Global Executives: The Lessons of International Experience*:

> An executive cannot learn cultural adaptability and the competencies associated with it without actually living and working in another culture and successfully coping with the accompanying discontinuities. This seems to be equally as true for Swedes as for French, for Americans as for Filipinos, for Malays as for Italians.

Start a school for global leaders.

We started a week-long course geared to serve the needs of global-level leaders who are new to their roles. This Global Leader Orientation provides a common learning community, with more seasoned global leaders serving as coaches for the program.

At this point you may be feeling overwhelmed. We have covered a lot of ground and set a very high standard for global leadership.

Don't lose heart! You are taking people to places they have never been before. You have never been there either.

God will use the challenge of your leadership role to change you before he will use you to change the world. This is God's method of growing the hearts of his leaders. The pressure is not on you. This is good news – this is the gospel – for you.

My prayer is that you will be encouraged where you are already leading well, and inspired to many of the fresh approaches put forth in these pages. Go for it!

We Must Stay Close

Our research probed the question: If a global leader has no more than five days per year of face-to-face time with his or her co-laborers in a multinational context, how can one appropriately serve, strengthen, inspire, align, equip, and coach those field leaders to live and lead well throughout the other 360 days?

Through this research process, leaders in our organization have been rediscovering the value of open dialogue—that you cannot just send an e-mail or discuss cultural values at an annual staff conference and expect changes of this nature to stick. It is not enough. Systemic change is a long-term process in which everyone must verbally engage.

William Isaacs explains why this dialogical approach is so important in *Dialogue and the Art of Thinking: A Pioneering Approach to Communicating in Business and in Life*: "The problems that even the most practical organizations have—in improving their performance and obtaining the results they desire—can be traced directly to their inability to think and talk together, particularly at critical moments." He continues:

Dialogue, as I define it here, is about a shared inquiry, a way of thinking and reflecting together. It is not something you do *to* another person. It is something you do *with* people. Indeed, a large part of learning this has to do with learning to shift your attitudes about relationships with others, so that we gradually give up the effort to make them understand us, and come to a greater understanding of ourselves and each other.

The ability to initiate this kind of dialogue will be a challenge for many leaders who were trained in a more traditional leadership model emphasizing the leader's role as direction setter, change agent, spokesperson, vision caster, and aligner. Taken at face value, the net result of these roles and responsibilities will produce a leadership bench full of one-way communicators who are always selling and not necessarily listening.

But the world is rapidly changing, and those who would seek to be part of shaping its future must understand the forces acting upon them. Leaders in all domains of society have realized that working alone cannot possibly solve stubborn problems such as poverty, AIDS, human trafficking, education, and malnutrition. Long-term solutions require collaboration with other entities over which these leaders exert little, if any, control.

Thus, the nature of governments, companies, organizations, and the global church is transforming from isolated hierarchical institutions to interdependent peer networks. Networks tend to be voluntary, informal, fluid, and relational. People contribute time, energy, and resources based on the perceived value of membership.

As missions leader Eddie Gibbs predicted in *Leadership Next: Changing Leaders in a Changing Culture*, "The new realities of postmodernity mean the future structure of the church must be fluid, flexible and capable of adjusting to diversity." Global leaders operating within these hierarchy-network hybrids can no longer rely on power, position, coercion, or financial incentives to exert influence.

They can, however, rely on principle-based practices that help them adapt to the variety of cultural settings global leaders encounter. They can also rely on the God of the nations who is deeply committed to glorifying himself among every tribe, tongue, people, and nation.

He has called us to lead close.

BIBLIOGRAPHY

Allen, Roland. *Missionary Methods: St. Paul's or Ours?* Grand Rapids, MI: William B. Eerdmans Publishing, 1962.

_____. *The Spontaneous Expansion of the Church and the Causes Which Hinder It*. Grand Rapids, MI: William B. Eerdmans Publishing, 1962.

Allen, David. *Getting Things Done: The Art of Stress-Free Productivity*. New York: Penguin Books, 2003.

Antonakis, John, and Leanne Atwater. "Leader Distance: A Proposed Theory." *The Leadership Quarterly* 13 (2002): 673-704.

Arndt, William, F. Wilbur Gingrich, Frederick W. Danker, and Walter Bauer. *A Greek-English Lexicon of the New Testament and Other Early Christian Literature*. 4th (Logos Bible Software) ed. Chicago: Logos Research Systems, 1996.

Avolio, B. J., F. O. Walumbwa, and T. J. Weber. "Leadership: Current Theories, Research, and Future Directions." *Annual Review of Psychology* 60 (2009): 421-49.

Bartlett, Christopher A., and Sumantra Ghoshal. "What Is a Global Manager?" *Harvard Business Review* 70, no. 5 (1992): 125.

Bass, Bernard M. *Leadership and Performance Beyond Expectations*. New York: Free Press, 1985.

Bass, Bernard M., and Ruth Bass. *The Bass Handbook of Leadership: Theory, Research, and Managerial Applications*. 4th ed. New York: Free Press, 2008.

Blackaby, Henry T., and Richard Blackaby. *Spiritual Leadership: Moving People on to God's Agenda*. Nashville, TN: Broadman and Holman Publishers, 2001.

Bock, Darrell L. *Acts* Baker Exegetical Commentary on the New Testament. Grand Rapids, MI: Baker Academic, 2007.

Borthwick, Paul. "Affirming Ethnic Identity, Combating Ethnocentricity: Foundations for Training Christian Leaders." D.Min. thesis, Gordon-Conwell Theological Seminary, 2007.

Bradner, Erin, Gloria Mark, and Tammie D. Hertel. "Team Size and Technology Fit: Participation, Awareness, and Rapport in Distributed Teams." *IEEE Transactions on Professional Communication* 48, no. 1 (2005).

Brafman, Ori, and Rod A. Beckstrom. *The Starfish and the Spider: The Unstoppable Power of Leaderless Organizations*. New York: Portfolio, 2006.

Burns, James MacGregor. *Leadership.* 1st ed. New York: Harper and Row, 1978.

Chhokar, Jagdeep Singh, Felix C. Brodbeck, Robert J. House, and Global Leadership and Organizational Behavior Effectiveness Research Program. *Culture and Leadership across the World: The Globe Book of in-Depth Studies of 25 Societies.* Mahwah, N.J.: Lawrence Erlbaum Associates, 2007.

Cisco. "A Study: Understanding and Managing the Mobile Workforce." *Cisco.* http://newsroom.cisco.com/dlls/2007/eKits/MobileWorkforce_071807.pdf [accessed October 20, 2011].

Clark, Randy, Leigh Anne Clark, and Katie Crossley. "Developing Multidimensional Trust without Touch in Virtual Teams." *Marketing Management Journal* 20, no. 1 (2010): 177-193.

Clemons, David, and Michael S. Kroth. *Managing the Mobile Workforce: Leading, Building, and Sustaining Virtual Teams.* New York: McGraw-Hill, 2011.

Collins, James C. *Good to Great: Why Some Companies Make the Leap—and Others Don't.* 1st ed. New York: HarperBusiness, 2001.

_____. "Good to Great and the Social Sectors: A Monograph to Accompany Good to Great." Boulder, CO: Jim Collins, 2005.

_____. *How the Mighty Fall: And Why Some Companies Never Give In.* New York: HarperCollins, 2009.

Connerley, Mary L., and Paul Pedersen. *Leadership in a Diverse and Multicultural Environment: Developing Awareness, Knowledge, and Skills.* Thousand Oaks, CA: Sage Publications, 2005.

Creswell, John W. *Qualitative Inquiry and Research Design: Choosing among Five Approaches.* 2nd ed. Thousand Oaks, CA: Sage Publications, 2007.

_____. *Research Design: Qualitative, Quantitative, and Mixed Methods Approaches.* 3rd ed. Thousand Oaks, CA: Sage Publications, 2009.

Daft, Richard L., and Patricia Lane. *The Leadership Experience.* 4th ed. Mason, OH: Thomson/South-Western, 2008.

Dalton, Maxine A., Chris Ernst, Jennifer Deal, and Jean Leslie. *Success for the New Global Manager: What You Need to Know to Work across Distances, Countries, and Cultures.* 1st ed. San Francisco: Jossey-Bass, 2002.

Denzin, Norman K., and Yvonna S. Lincoln, eds. *The Sage Handbook of Qualitative Research.* Thousand Oaks: Sage Publications, 2005.

Dierendonck, Dirk van, and Kathleen Patterson. *Servant Leadership: Developments in Theory and Research.* New York: Palgrave Macmillan, 2010.

Dorfman, Peter W., Paul J. Hanges, and Felix C. Brodbeck. "Leadership and Cultural Variation: The Identification of Culturally Endorsed Leadership Profiles." In *Culture, Leadership, and Organizations: The Globe Study of 62 Societies,* edited by Robert J.

House, Paul J. Hanges, Mansour Javidian, Peter W. Dorfman and Vipin Gupta. Thousand Oaks, CA: Sage, 2004.

Dorfman, Peter W., and Robert J. House. "Cultural Influences on Organizational Leadership." In *Culture, Leadership, and Organizations: The Globe Study of 62 Societies*, edited by Robert J. House, Paul J. Hanges, Mansour Javidian, Peter W. Dorfman and Vipin Gupta. Thousand Oaks, CA: Sage, 2004.

Drucker, Peter. *Managing the Nonprofit Organization*. New York: HarperCollins, 1990.

Easton, Matthew G. *Easton's Bible Dictionary*. Oak Harbor, WA: Logos Research Systems, Inc., 1996.

Eshleman, Paul. "World Evangelization in the 21st Century." In *Cape Town 2010: Lausanne*. Cape Town, South Africa, 2010.

Fry, Louis. "Toward a Theory of Spiritual Leadership." *The Leadership Quarterly* 14, no. 6 (2003): 693-727.

Gaebelein, Frank Ely, J. D. Douglas, and Dick Polcyn. *The Expositor's Bible Commentary, Volume 2: Genesis - Numbers*. 14 vols. Logos electronic ed. Grand Rapids, MI: Zondervan, 1995.

Getz, Gene A. *Elders and Leaders: God's Plan for Leading the Church—a Biblical, Historical, and Cultural Perspective*. Chicago: Moody Publishers, 2003.

Gibbs, Eddie. *Leadership Next: Changing Leaders in a Changing Culture*. Downers Grove, IL: InterVarsity Press, 2005.

Goldsmith, Marshall, Cathy Greenberg, Alastair Robertson, and Maya Hu-Chan. *Global Leadership: The Next Generation*. Upper Saddle River, NJ: FT/Prentice Hall, 2003.

Goleman, Daniel. "What Makes a Leader?" *Harvard Business Review*, no. Nov-Dec (1998): 92-102.

Graen, George B., and Mary Uhl-Bien. "Relationship-Based Approach to Leadership: Development of Leader-Member Exchange (Lmx) Theory of Leadership over 25 Years: Applying a Multi-Level Multi-Domain Perspective." *The Leadership Quarterly* 6, no. 2 (1995): 219-247.

Greenleaf, Robert K., and Larry C. Spears. *The Power of Servant Leadership*. San Francisco: Berrett-Koehler Publishers, 1998.

Greenleaf, Robert K., Larry C. Spears, and Stephen R. Covey. *Servant Leadership: A Journey into the Nature of Legitimate Power and Greatness*. Mahwah, NJ: Paulist Press, 2002.

Greenslade, Philip. *Leadership, Greatness and Servanthood*. Minneapolis, MN: Bethany House Publishers, 1984.

Grenny, Joseph. "Virtual Teams Keep People Connected." *Leadership Excellence*, May 2010, 20.

Grogan, Geoffrey W. "Isaiah." In *The Expositor's Bible Commentary, Volume 6: Isaiah - Ezekiel*, edited by Frank Ely Gaebelein, J. D. Douglas and Dick Polcyn Grand Rapids, MI: Zondervan, 1995.

Groh, Greg Robert. "Convergence: Missiology, Ecclesiology and Spiritual Leadership in the 21st Century." Denver, CO: Worldwide Leadership Council, 1998.

Gundling, Ernest. *Working Globesmart: 12 People Skills for Doing Business across Borders.* 1st ed. Palo Alto, CA: Davies-Black Pub., 2003.

Hahn, Geoffrey W. "Cross-Cultural Partnerships Characterized by Grace." D.Min. thesis, Denver Seminary, 2007.

Hammer, Michael, and Lisa W. Hershman. *Faster, Cheaper, Better.* Kindle ed. New York: Crown Business, 2010.

Herr, Kathryn, and Gary L. Anderson. *The Action Research Dissertation: A Guide for Students and Faculty.* Thousand Oaks, CA: SAGE Publications, 2005.

Hesselbein, Frances, Marshall Goldsmith, and Leader to Leader Institute. *The Organization of the Future 2: Visions, Strategies, and Insights on Managing in a New Era.* 1st, Kindle ed. San Francisco: Jossey-Bass, 2009.

Hickman, Gill Robinson. *Leading Organizations: Perspectives for a New Era.* 2nd ed. Los Angeles: SAGE Publications, 2010.

Hiebert, Paul G. *Anthropological Insights for Missionaries.* Grand Rapids, MI: Baker Book House, 1985.

Hirsch, Alan. *The Forgotten Ways: Reactivating the Missional Church.* Grand Rapids, MI: Brazos Press, 2006.

Hofstede, Geert H. *Culture's Consequences: Comparing Values, Behaviors, Institutions, and Organizations across Nations.* 2nd ed. Thousand Oaks, CA: Sage Publications, 2001.

Hofstede, Geert H., Gert Jan Hofstede, and Michael Minkov. *Cultures and Organizations: Software of the Mind: Intercultural Cooperation and Its Importance for Survival.* 3rd ed. New York: McGraw-Hill, 2010.

The Holy Bible, English Standard Version. Wheaton, IL: Crossway, 2001.

House, R. J., P. J. Hanges, M. Javidan, P. W. Dorfman, and V. Gupta. *Culture, Leadership, and Organizations: The Globe Study of 62 Societies.* Thousand Oaks, CA: Sage Publications, 2004.

Hunter, James C. *The Servant: A Simple Story About the True Essence of Leadership.* Rocklin, CA: Prima Pub., 1998.

Irving, Justin A. "Decentralization and the Shared Leadership of the New Testament." Minneapolis, MN: Bethel University, 2004.

Isaacs, William. *Dialogue and the Art of Thinking Together: A Pioneering Approach to Communicating in Business and in Life.* 1st ed. New York: Currency, 1999.

Ismail, Kiran M., and David L. Ford. "Organizational Leadership in Central Asia and the Caucasus: Research Considerations and Directions." *Asia Pacific Journal of Management* 2010, no. 27 (2010): 321-340.

Katzenbach, Jon R., and Douglas K. Smith. *The Wisdom of Teams: Creating the High-Performance Organization.* New York: HarperBusiness Essentials, 2003.

Kayworth, Timothy R., and Dorothy E. Leidner. "Leadership Effectiveness in Global Virtual Teams." *Journal of Management Information Systems* 18, no. 3 (2002): 7-40.

Klenke, Karin, ed. *Qualitative Research in the Study of Leadership.* Bingley, UK: Emerald Group, 2008.

Kling, Fritz. *The Meeting of the Waters: 7 Global Currents That Will Propel the Future Church.* 1st, Kindle ed. Colorado Springs, CO: David C. Cook, 2010.

Kostenberger, Andreas J., and Peter T. O'Brien. *Salvation to the Ends of the Earth.* Downers Grove, IL: InterVarsity Press, 2001.

Kotter, John. "Hierarchy and Network: Two Structures, One Organization." *Harvard Business Review blog.* http://blogs.hbr.org/kotter/2011/05/two-structures-one-organizatio.html [accessed May 26, 2011].

Kouzes, James M., and Barry Z. Posner. *The Leadership Challenge.* 4th ed. San Francisco: Jossey-Bass, 2007.

_____. *The Truth About Leadership: The No-Fads, Heart-of-the-Matter Facts You Need to Know.* 1st, Kindle ed. San Francisco: Jossey-Bass, 2010.

LaFasto, Frank M. J., and Carl E. Larson. *When Teams Work Best: 6,000 Team Members and Leaders Tell What It Takes to Succeed*. Thousand Oaks, CA: Sage Publications, 2001.

Laub, Jim. "From Paternalism to the Servant Organization: Expanding the Organizational Leadership Assessment Model." *Proceedings of the 2003 Servant Leadership Research Roundtable* (2003).

Lencioni, Patrick. *The Five Dysfunctions of a Team: A Leadership Fable*. 1st ed. San Francisco: Jossey-Bass, 2002.

Lewis, Richard D. *When Cultures Collide: Leading across Cultures*. Kindle 3rd ed. Boston: Nicholas Brealey International, 2005.

Li, Charlene. *Open Leadership: How Social Technology Can Transform the Way You Lead*. 1st ed. San Francisco: Jossey-Bass, 2010.

Linden, Russell Matthew. *Leading across Boundaries: Creating Collaborative Agencies in a Networked World*. 1st ed. San Francisco: Jossey-Bass, 2010.

Lingenfelter, Sherwood G., and Marvin Keene Mayers. *Ministering Cross-Culturally: An Incarnational Model for Personal Relationships*. 2nd ed. Grand Rapids, MI: Baker Academic, 2003.

Lipnack, Jessica, and Jeffrey Stamps. *Virtual Teams: People Working across Boundaries with Technology*. 2nd ed. New York: Wiley, 2000.

Lucas, Kevin A. "Examining Servant Leadership within Virtual and Face-to-Face Teams." PhD diss., Regent University, 2007.

MacMillan, Pat. *The Performance Factor: Unlocking the Secrets of Teamwork.* Nashville, TN: Broadman and Holman Publishers, 2001.

Mahbubani, Kishore. *Beyond the Age of Innocence: Rebuilding Trust between America and the World.* New York: Public Affairs, 2005.

Manz, Charles C., and Henry P. Sims, Jr. "Superleadership: Beyond the Myth of Heroic Leadership." In *The Leader's Companion: Insights on Leadership through the Ages*, edited by J. Thomas Wren, 212-221. New York: Free Press, 1995.

Marquardt, Michael J., and Lisa Horvath. *Global Teams: How Top Multinationals Span Boundaries and Cultures with High-Speed Teamwork.* 1st ed. Palo Alto, CA: Davies-Black Pub., 2001.

Marshall, Tom. *Understanding Leadership.* Kent, England: Sovereign World, 1991.

Martin, Ted, and Michael Cozzens. *Principles of Leadership: What We Can Learn from the Life and Ministry of Bill Bright.* Orlando, FL: NewLife Publications, 2001.

Matteson, Jeffrey A. "The Emergence of Self-Sacrificial Leadership: An Exploration of the Theoretical Boundaries from the Perspective of the Leader." PhD diss., Regent University, 2006.

Matteson, Jeffrey A., and Justin A. Irving. "Servant Versus Self-Sacrificial Leadership: A Behavioral Comparison of Two Follower-Oriented Leadership Theories." *International Journal of Leadership Studies* 2, no. 1 (2006): 36-51.

McCall, Morgan W., and George P. Hollenbeck. *Developing Global Executives: The Lessons of International Experience.* Boston: Harvard Business School Press, 2002.

McDermott, Lynda C., Nolan Brawley, and William W. Waite. *World Class Teams: Working across Borders.* New York: Wiley, 1998.

McNeal, Reggie. *Missional Renaissance: Changing the Scorecard for the Church.* 1st ed. San Francisco: Jossey-Bass, 2009.

Meyer, Christian. *Leadership Influence and Distance: Energizing an Organization across Geographic and Ethnic-Cultural Distance.* Saarbrucken, Germany: VDM Verlag, 2007.

Miles, Matthew B., and A. M. Huberman. *Qualitative Data Analysis: An Expanded Sourcebook.* 2nd ed. Thousand Oaks, CA: Sage Publications, 1994.

Morse, MaryKate. *Making Room for Leadership: Power, Space and Influence.* Downers Grove, IL: IVP Books, 2008.

Napier, Barbara J., and Gerald R. Ferris. "Distance in Organizations." *Human Resource Management Review* 3, no. 4 (1993): 321-357.

Nemiro, Jill E. *The Handbook of High-Performance Virtual Teams: A Toolkit for Collaborating across Boundaries.* 1st ed. San Francisco: Jossey-Bass, 2008.

Nisbett, Richard E. *The Geography of Thought: How Asians and Westerners Think Differently—and Why.* New York: Free Press, 2003.

Northouse, Peter G. *Leadership: Theory and Practice*. 4th ed. Thousand Oaks, CA: Sage Publications, 2006.

Nurmi, Niina. "Coping with Coping Strategies: How Distributed Teams and Their Members Deal with the Stress of Distance, Time Zones and Culture." *Stress and Health* 27, no. 2 (2011): 123-143.

OfficingToday. "Can Your Business Center Serve the 1 Billion-Plus Mobile Workers?" *Officing Today*. http://www.officingtoday.com/index.php?news=703 [accessed October 28, 2011].

Page, Don. *Servant-Empowered Leadership: A Hands-on Guide to Transforming You and Your Organization*. Langley, BC, Canada: Power To Change Ministries, 2009.

Panteli, Niki, and Robert Tucker. "Power and Trust in Global Virtual Teams." *Communications of the ACM* 52, no. 12 (2009): 113.

Parker, Glenn M. *Cross-Functional Teams: Working with Allies, Enemies, and Other Strangers*. 2nd ed. San Francisco: Jossey-Bass, 2003.

Patterson, Kathleen. "Servant Leadership: A Theoretical Model." PhD diss., Regent University, 2003.

Pearce, Craig L., and Jay Alden Conger. *Shared Leadership: Reframing the Hows and Whys of Leadership*. Thousand Oaks: Sage Publications, 2003.

Pellegrini, Ekin K., Terri A. Scandura, and Vaidyanathan Jayaraman. "Cross-Cultural Generalizability of Paternalistic Leadership:

An Expansion of Leader-Member Exchange Theory." *Group and Organization Management* 35, no. 4 (2010): 391-420.

Peterson, Eugene H. *Under the Unpredictable Plant: An Exploration in Vocational Holiness.* Kindle ed. Grand Rapids, MI: W.B. Eerdmans, 1992.

_____. *The Jesus Way: A Conversation on the Ways That Jesus Is the Way.* Grand Rapids, MI: William B. Eerdmans Pub., 2007.

Piper, John. *Let the Nations Be Glad!: The Supremacy of God in Missions.* Grand Rapids, MI: Baker Books, 1993.

Plueddemann, James C. *Leading across Cultures: Effective Ministry and Mission in the Global Church.* Downers Grove, IL: IVP Academic, 2009.

Rath, Tom, and Barry Conchie. *Strengths Based Leadership.* New York: Gallup Press, 2008.

Reason, Peter, and Hilary Bradbury, eds. *The Sage Handbook of Action Research: Participative Inquiry and Practice.* London ; Thousand Oaks, CA: SAGE Publications, 2008.

Rhoads, Mohja. "Face-to-Face and Computer-Mediated Communication: What Does Theory Tell Us and What Have We Learned So Far?" *Journal of Planning Literature* 25, no. 2 (2010): 111-122.

Riggio, R. E., I. Chaleff, and J. Lipman-Blumen. *The Art of Followership: How Great Followers Create Great Leaders and Organizations.* San Francisco: Jossey-Bass, 2008.

Rinehart, Stacy. *Upside Down: The Paradox of Servant Leadership.* Colorado Springs, Colo.: NavPress, 1998.

Robert, Lionel P., Alan R. Denis, and Yu-Ting Caisy Hung. "Individual Swift Trust and Knowledge-Based Trust in Face-to-Face and Virtual Team Members." *Journal of Management Information Systems* 26, no. 2 (2009): 241-279.

Rosinski, Philippe. *Coaching across Cultures: New Tools for Leveraging National, Corporate, and Professional Differences.* London: Nicholas Brealey Pub., 2003.

Roussin, Christopher J. "Increasing Trust, Psychological Safety, and Team Performance through Dyadic Leadership Discovery." *Small Group Research* 39, no. 2 (2008): 224-248-224-248.

Sanders, J. Oswald. *Spiritual Leadership: Principles of Excellence for Every Believer.* Chicago: Moody Publishers, 2007.

Schein, Edgar H. *Organizational Culture and Leadership.* 4th ed. San Francisco: Jossey-Bass, 2010.

Schnabel, Eckhard J. *Paul the Missionary: Realities, Strategies and Methods.* Downers Grove, IL: IVP Academic, 2008.

Schreiner, Thomas R. *Paul, Apostle of God's Glory in Christ: A Pauline Theology.* Leicester, England: Apollos, 2001.

Serrano, Magdo. "Servant Leadership: A Viable Model for the Panamanian Context?" PhD diss., Regent University, 2006.

Shirey, William J. "Leader-Follower Communication in the 21st Century: How Distractions Can Influence Relationships." PhD diss., Regent University, 2007.

Solomon, Charlene Marmer, and Michael S. Schell. *Managing across Cultures: The Seven Keys to Doing Business with a Global Mindset.* New York: McGraw-Hill, 2009.

Spears, Larry C., and Michele Lawrence. *Focus on Leadership: Servant Leadership for the Twenty-First Century.* New York: J. Wiley and Sons, 2002.

Stewart, Greg L., Charles C. Manz, and Henry P. Sims. *Team Work and Group Dynamics.* New York: J. Wiley, 1999.

Stone, A. G., R. F. Russell, and K. Patterson. "Transformational Versus Servant Leadership: A Difference in Leader Focus." *Leadership and Organization Development Journal* 25, no. 4 (2004): 349-361.

Swanson, James. *Dictionary of Biblical Languages with Semantic Domains: Hebrew (Old Testament).* Logos electronic ed. Oak Harbor, WA: Logos Research Systems, Inc., 1997.

Swindoll, Charles R. *Paul: A Man of Grace and Grit.* Nashville, TN: Word Publishing Group, 2002.

Taylor, Bill. "Where Have All the Business Heroes Gone?". http://blogs.hbr.org/taylor/2010/07/where_have_all_the_business_he.html [accessed October 15, 2011].

TowersWatson. *Shaping Our Future Together: Culture Change Analyses and Results, Executive Team Presentation*. Orlando, FL: Campus Crusade for Christ, August 2010.

Ware, James. "Managing People You Can't See: Connecting and Engaging Distributed Teams." *The Future of Work*. http://resources. idgenterprise.com/original/AST-0043723_Managing_People_ You_Can_t_See.pdf [accessed October 13, 2011].

Weisband, Suzanne P. *Leadership at a Distance: Research in Technologically-Supported Work*. New York: Lawrence Erlbaum Associates, 2008.

Wheatley, Margaret J. *Leadership and the New Science: Discovering Order in a Chaotic World*. 3rd ed. San Francisco: Berrett-Koehler, 2006.

Winston, Bruce. *Be a Leader for God's Sake: From Values to Behaviors*. Virginia Beach, VA: Regent University School of Leadership Studies, 2002.

Winter, Ralph D., Steven C. Hawthorne, Darrell R. Dorr, D. Bruce Graham, and Bruce A. Koch. *Perspectives on the World Christian Movement: A Reader*. 4th ed. Pasadena, CA: William Carey Library, 2009.

Wright, Christopher J. H. *The Mission of God: Unlocking the Bible's Grand Narrative*. Downers Grove, IL: IVP Academic, 2006.

Yan, Jun, and James G. Jerry Hunt. "A Cross Cultural Perspective on Perceived Leadership Effectiveness." *International Journal of Cross Cultural Management* 5, no. 1 (2005): 49-66.

Yukl, Gary. *Leadership in Organizations*. 7th ed. Upper Saddle River, NJ: Prentice Hall, 2010.

Zimmermann, Angelika. "Interpersonal Relationships in Transnational, Virtual Teams: Towards a Configurational Perspective." *International Journal of Management Reviews* 13, no. 1 (2011): 59-78.

ACKNOWLEDGEMENTS

First and foremost, "I thank him who has given me strength, Christ Jesus our Lord, because he judged me faithful, appointing me to his service" (1 Timothy 1:12).

A research-grounded book of this scope is impossible to complete alone. I am deeply indebted to those who have walked the path with me. I want to thank my best friend and wife, Ann, who proved a constant source of encouragement, inspiration, and wisdom as she tirelessly listened to my ideas. I am also grateful to my adult children, Travis and Amy, who empathized with the evenings and weekends I devoted to reading and writing.

I want to thank my doctoral advisors, Dr. Jeffrey Matteson and Dr. Justin Irving, for their availability and practical wisdom. I also appreciate Dr. Irving's vision for servant leadership and that he practices what he preaches.

I want to thank my fellow staff members at Cru/Campus Crusade for Christ. Their patience, enthusiasm, and understanding gave me the support I needed. They have invested their lives in making disciples of the nations; I have learned much from their examples of loving leadership. I am particularly grateful for our president Dr. Steve Douglass, his friendship, and his whole-hearted support of this project. My devotion to this project also cost the teams on which I serve. I appreciate the encouragement they offered along the way.

Finally, I want to thank many people who served me in the writing process. Claire Angus, my executive assistant, provided invaluable help in collating interviews, typing transcripts, and organizing field research data into manageable pieces. Andy Butcher, Gina Butz, Gary Runn, Ben and Linda Sparkman, and Matt Watts spent many hours proofreading and editing my drafts. While any errors are mine, the quality of this work is far greater because of their assistance.

ABOUT THE AUTHOR

Ken Cochrum (DMin, Bethel University) is Vice President of Global Digital Strategies at Cru (formerly Campus Crusade for Christ) in Orlando, Florida. An avid cyclist and aspiring guitarist, he also holds a degree in Mechanical Engineering from The University of Texas and a Masters of Arts in Biblical Studies from Dallas Theological Seminary. He recently co-founded Indigitous.org, a movement passionate about connecting people to Jesus using digital strategies. He previously served as vice president of Cru's student-led movements worldwide. He and his wife Ann spent 13 years as missionaries in East Asia where they raised their two children. Ken blogs regularly at www.onleadingwell.com.

Made in the USA
San Bernardino, CA
24 December 2013